CUT TO THE CHASE

Stuart R. Levine, former CEO of Dale Carnegie & Associates, Inc., is Chairman and CEO of Stuart Levine & Associates LLC, a consulting and leadership development company. Author of the national bestseller *The Six Fundamentals of Success* and co-author of the international bestseller *The Leader in You*, he has spoken throughout Europe, the Pacific Rim, and South America. He has been profiled in leading publications and has made numerous television appearances to discuss leadership and personal growth. He serves as Lead Director for Gentiva Health Services, Inc. and J. D'Addario & Company, Inc. and has been frequently called on to discuss corporate governance issues.

Praise for *Cut to the Chase*

'*Cut to the Chase* offers 100 very useful managerial ideas in compact, punchy form. It's terrific!' **Josh Weston, Honorary Chairman of the Board, Automatic Data Processing, Inc.**

'Stuart Levine's rules get results. This is a book to be read, re-read, and most of all, used.' **Jim D'Addario, Chairman and CEO, J. D'Addario & Company, Inc.**

'Extremely valuable advice on the importance of clear, intelligent communication and action. I only wish I had this book 20 years ago!' **Sam Williamson, Vice President, Systems & Technology Group, Americas IBM**

'Time is our most limited resource. This sensational book will help you to use your time wisely, to achieve success as you define it.' **Henry A. Sheinkopf, President, Sheinkopf Ltd**

'*Cut to the Chase* tells you how to work and live more productively - and achieve a happier, more fulfilling life.' **Dr Gregory H. Williams, President, The City College of New York and author of *Life on the Color Line***

'If your goal is to be more responsive to client needs, get desired results, and lead a more productive life, read this invaluable book.' **Paul D. McKinnis, Senior Client Partner, Korn Ferry International**

'PAC or "point accepted" is but one of the time-saving tools Stuart Levine has shared that we use every day to keep communication crisp and moving along.' **Ronald A. Malone, Chairman and CEO, Gentiva Health Services**

'In selling, time is money; you must be able to express yourself in clear terms. This book is a career home run.' **Charles Shor, President and CEO, Duro Bag Manufacturing Company**

'Achieving balance is the key to success in life! And at heart, that is what Levine's "cut to the chase" message is all about.' **Richard A. Loughlin, Vice Chairman, Willis Risk Solutions, North America**

'A perfect bulls-eye. Sharp, practical, to-the-point advice for success in business and life.' **Matthew T. Crosson, President, Long Island Association, Inc.**

CUT
TO THE
CHASE

AND 99 OTHER RULES
TO LIBERATE YOURSELF AND
GAIN BACK THE GIFT OF TIME

STUART R. LEVINE

BUSINESS
BOOKS

Published by Random House Business Books 2007

2 4 6 8 10 9 7 5 3 1

Copyright © Stuart R. Levine 2007

Stuart R. Levine has asserted his right under the Copyright, Designs
and Patents Act 1988 to be identified as the author of this work

First published in the United States in 2006 by
Doubleday, an imprint of The Doubleday Broadway
Publishing Group, a division of Random House, Inc.,
New York.

Random House Business Books
Random House, 20 Vauxhall Bridge Road,
London SW1V 2SA

www.randomhouse.co.uk

Addresses for companies within The Random House Group Limited can
be found at: www.randomhouse.co.uk/offices.htm

The Random House Group Limited Reg. No. 954009

A CIP catalogue record for this book is
available from the British Library

ISBN 9781905211418

The Random House Group Limited makes every effort to ensure that the
papers used in its books are made from trees that have been legally
sourced from well-managed and credibly certified forests.
Our paper procurement policy can be found at:
www.randomhouse.co.uk/paper.htm

Printed in the UK by CPI Bookmarque, Croydon, CR0 4YY

To Harriet—energetic, passionate and loving
To Jesse—a living expression of strength, and values
To Elizabeth—clear, thoughtful, and purposeful

You each inspire me every day. Making more time to spend with you is what cutting to the chase is all about.

ACKNOWLEDGMENTS

Thanks to my literary agent, Martha Jewett, who was a critical resource to me throughout this process. I also want to thank Roger Scholl and Sarah Rainone of Doubleday for their dedicated effort. Special thanks, too, to my colleague Sally Allen whose steady sense of purpose and focus on adding value for the reader was a driving energy for me. Bryan Fryzel, thanks for your attitude and responsive nature. To Ronald Malone, Larry Tarica, and Jack Leahy—your continuing candor in reviewing this material was deeply appreciated.

My thoughts on this critical topic have been shaped by professional and personal interactions with many smart, insightful people—too many to list—but I would like to acknowledge and thank those who directly influenced this work: Jon Cohen, Jim D'Addario, Rich Daly, Wayne Grosse, Shaygan Kheradpir, Kirk Kordeleski, Thomas J. McAteer Jr., Giovanni Meccariello, Weston Milliken, Christopher J. L. O'Connell, James Orsini, Wallace Parker, Laura Peddy, John Rubadeau, Raymond S. Troubh, Doonie and Betty Waldron, Sam Williamson, Josh Weston.

I would also like to honor my sister-in-law, Adrienne Bernard, who has taught me a great deal this year about the value of life and the importance of treasuring each moment.

Also by Stuart R. Levine

The Six Fundamentals of Success

CONTENTS

PREFACE   xiii

START NOW!

  1. Cut to the Chase.   1

  2. Just start.   3

  3. Get in early and go home on time.   5

  4. I got it.   7

  5. The first twenty minutes.   9

  6. You're killing me.   11

  7. Get over it.   13

  8. It's not always about you.   15

  9. What's keeping you up at night?   17

10. Don't hide your passion.   19

THINK CLEARLY

11. Start with the end in mind.   21

12. Focus on one thing at a time.   23

13. Organize yourself *first*. 25

14. Assumptions kill. 27

15. Think in bullets. 29

16. Trust your gut. 31

17. Predict how long things will take. 33

18. Tailor your message to your audience. 35

19. What's been going better lately—and why? 38

SPEED UP

20. Explode out of the blocks. 41

21. Every second counts. 43

22. Know how things really get done. 45

23. Build momentum. 47

24. Make sure your handoffs are clean. 50

25. Bag consensus. 52

26. Break through silos. 54

27. Appeal to their enlightened self-interest. 56

28. Measure twice, cut once. 58

29. Close the loop. 60

30. Call an audible. 62

31. Beat change to the punch. 64

32. To speed up, slow down. 66

BE DIRECT

33. Teach people how to use your time. 69

34. Treat others' time as you would your own. 71

35. Know what's being asked of you. 73

36. If you want something, ask for it. 75

37. Tell them if the baby is ugly. 77

38. Cut to the chase without drawing blood. 79

39. Make sure everyone has the map. 81

40. Tell them what's on the test. 83

41. Know your work style—and theirs. 85

42. Clear the air. 87

43. Cut the bull. 89

44. Create a "no loitering" zone. 91

45. You can't please everyone. 93

MEET SMARTER

46. People hate meetings for a reason. 95

47. Every conversation should have a purpose. 97

48. 120 seconds and out. 99

49. Know when you're not needed. 101

50. Master the ten-minute meeting. 103

51. Count noses. 105

52. Stay on course. 107

53. Don't grandstand. 109

54. Have a meeting before the meeting. 111

55. Debrief. 113

56. Stay in touch. 115

57. Master the graceful exit. 118

58. Recognize when it's all been said. 120

MOVE FORWARD

59. Look at the big picture. 121

60. Know your weaknesses, but play to your strengths. 123

61. Think three moves ahead. 125

62. Know when your career is stuck. 127

63. Make opportunity happen. 129

64. Delegate. 131

65. Life is a negotiation. 133

66. Know when to wait. 135

67. Know when *not* to wait. 137

68. If you need a drummer, hire a drummer. 139

69. Don't be afraid to hire people you're going to lose. 141

CUT BACK

70. Decide what not to do. 143

71. Addition by subtraction. 145

72. Rip it in half. 147

73. The highlighter is mightier than the sword. 149

74. A picture is worth a thousand words. 151

75. Tell a story. 153

76. On it. Pending. Done. 155

77. . . . To get to the other side. 157

78. Weed out your reading pile. 159

79. TMI (too much information). 161

80. Good enough is good enough. 163

WATCH OUT

81. Your time is your life. 165

82. Don't let your BlackBerry become a CrackBerry. 167

83. Avoid toxic people. 169

84. Don't let distractions derail you. 171

85. Don't hang in the door and chat. 173

86. Cut down on the fire drills. 175

87. Know when you're stuck. 177

88. When you hear something once, pay attention.
When you hear it twice, act. 179

89. If you sense trouble, do something. 181

90. Procrastination takes years off your life. 183

91. Don't confuse activity with accomplishment. 185

92. Don't make the same mistake twice. 187

93. Sweat the small stuff. 189

FIND BALANCE

94. Don't let a difficult coworker dominate your life. 191

95. Manage your personal life as well as your
professional life. 193

96. Renew yourself every day. 195

97. Take back the weekend. 197

98. Turn the page. 199

99. Know when to put the book down. 201

100. A bottle of wine, a cut flower. 203

Move past the page and into action. 205

Calendar 207

Before appearing on the *Today* show to discuss my previous book, *The Six Fundamentals of Success*, I was talking to Matt Lauer about some of the ideas in the book. Right before we went on the air, he leaned over and said, "You know what really drives me nuts? When people come into my office for a five-minute conversation and, an hour later, *they're still there*! Why can't they *cut to the chase*?"

Matt was among the first to single out that rule, but he was not the last. In countless conversations with CEOs and managers, in my speaking engagements and in my consulting work with executives at some of the top companies in the country, I heard similar questions: How can I get people to stop wasting my time? How can I keep conversations on track? How can I get more done in less time?

They all boiled down to the same answer: by cutting to the chase.

Cutting to the chase is about much more than getting to the point. It's about *defining your purpose*—whether in accomplishing a specific task or in your career and life. It's about *knowing your world*—your job, your organization, your industry—and your place in it. It's about *concentrating*—shutting out distractions, setting personal boundaries, and focusing on your goals. Ultimately, it's about understanding that your time is, quite literally, your life.

The rules that follow are lessons that I've learned from my decades of working with managers and executives. You can apply these lessons to your own life and career, no matter what your job or how high up in your organization you are—or hope to be. This book will help you as individuals and leaders, as family members and community members, to continually reinforce the purposefulness of your actions. Nothing, I would argue, translates more directly into effective performance. But these rules aren't only for individuals; companies, too, benefit from cutting to the chase. In fact, I believe helping people cut to the chase is the critical leadership skill of the next decade.

I believe that each of the 100 rules in this book is essential and have avoided repetition whenever possible. However, you will find recurring themes—keeping meetings short, conversations focused, and communication clear.

Ideas as important as these bear repeating in different contexts and applications.

Whether the waters ahead are calm or turbulent, people who cut to the chase are the ones who will thrive. Because cutting to the chase isn't just about doing your work faster—it's about putting your career on the fast track. It will lead to better business results—and liberate you to focus on everything you're working *for:* your community, hobbies and avocations, and, most important, the people you love.

While the payoff for cutting to the chase is more time, ironically, it often requires you to invest some time and energy up front. As with any type of personal training, it requires discipline, practice, and heart. I suggest tackling a few rules to start that speak best to your situation. Take note of how much time they help you to save—I promise that you'll be invigorated by the results.

Life is beautiful and fragile. The disasters that have rocked our world in the early twenty-first century have, I believe, led people to a greater awareness of that fact. We live in an age where our competitiveness is matched only by our desire for work/life balance. Of course, at the same time employees are striving for greater meaning in their lives, employers are struggling to create increased value for customers and shareholders. How do you solve these seemingly conflicting problems? By defining your purpose, knowing your world, and concentrating. In other words, by cutting to the chase.

I'd enjoy hearing your experiences applying these rules. Please e-mail me at cuttothechase@stuartlevine.com. You can also visit our Web site at www.stuartlevine.com. Thank you.

—Stuart R. Levine

Start Now!

1. Cut to the Chase.

The only rule I have repeated from my previous book, *The Six Fundamentals of Success,* is Cut to the Chase. Why the need to say more here? And why an entire book on the subject? Because I realized that my prior advice only scratched the surface of what cutting to the chase is all about.

We give our time away all day long, to emotions that gain us no advantages, to people who do not value our time, to inefficient habits. If you want to take back this time, you need to cut to the chase. The following are the underlying principles behind cutting to the chase, and, in fact, every one of the other ninety-nine rules in the book.

1) *Define your purpose*. Whether you're planning a major project at work or thinking about where you want to

be in ten years, a clear purpose is your true north by which to navigate as conditions change.

2) *Know your world.* Continuously seek to understand what's happening in the world, the economy, your industry, and your organization. Recognize what motivates people. And most important, know yourself—and the world around you.

3) *Concentrate.* Shut out distractions. Set personal boundaries. Focus. Don't let people steal your time and don't give it away easily.

Cutting to the chase means approaching everything from your next phone call to the next five years of your career with clarity and focus. It's about knowing what's important and what's not. It's about spending time wisely—yours and others'. It's about getting more done with less effort. And, yes, it's also about work/life balance—about taking back the weekends and leaving work earlier so you can spend more time doing things you enjoy with the ones you love.

Cutting to the chase involves a commitment to thinking differently. It's easy to blame change, intrusive technologies, or increasing expectations at work for our own lack of discipline. But wasting time is a personal choice. You can continue complaining that you never have enough time. Or you can put down your BlackBerry, switch off your e-mail alarm, close your office door, take a deep breath, turn the page . . . and just start.

2. Just start.

Whatever you can do or dream you can, begin it. Boldness has genius, power and magic in it!

—Goethe

The longer you delay starting something, the more shadows you see. To paraphrase a famous Nike campaign, *just start.*

One CEO I know wanted to initiate a recognition program called "I Caught You Doing Something Good." He created a committee to put the program together. But the people on it were busy with their regular jobs and had trouble finding the time to meet. The CEO was anxious to spend more time recognizing his people for their hard work. Realizing that the committee was too swamped to put the program together in a timely fashion, he just started. He sent an e-mail to the entire management team asking for nominations. When the results were in, he sent his high performers a personal thank-you note and a $100 gift certificate. The program is working beautifully. The energy it created has added momentum to the company.

Wouldn't it be nice if life took a cue from horse racing and a gun went off when it was time for us to get moving? Life rarely sends us a signal as clear as a starter's pistol. It's up to us to recognize when it's time to just start.

3. Get in early and go home on time.

Too many people get to work fifteen minutes late, thinking they'll stay late to make up the lost time. They spend the first half hour getting coffee and catching up with colleagues on the hot new reality TV show. Once they sit down, they make a couple of personal phone calls, and if they're lucky, they'll get in an hour or so of "real work" before lunch. Of course, lunch itself is split between planning an upcoming meeting at their desks and catching up on office gossip. With the rest of the day spent returning e-mails, they might get in two or three hours of real work. So they stay late, inevitably chatting with the other night owls for another half an hour. But it's okay—after all, they're "off the clock."

These people leave the office hours later than they should. They feel burned out because they've been there for almost ten hours, crammed in lunch at their desks, and still have so much left to do. Such people often feel ill-used by the organization and see themselves as martyrs. But the truth is, they have wasted hours of valuable work time and have accomplished far less than they could have.

The most effective executives and aspiring executives and managers get in early and stay focused all day. To regain control of your day, first get to work on time. Or, better yet, early. Work smart and hard the entire time you're there. Visualize a stopwatch ticking away in your head, if necessary. At lunch, leave the office—if only for five or ten minutes—to clear your head so you can be productive in the afternoon. If you want to catch up with friends at the office, schedule lunch with them. When colleagues drop by your office, tell them, "I'm working on something right now, but I'd love to catch up. Why don't we schedule lunch?"

Don't confuse time spent at the office with time spent working productively. Working hard and smart will liberate you to spend more time *outside* the office with the people you care about most.

4. I got it.

As soon as you understand exactly what someone is explaining, tell them in one way or another, "I got it." Doing so frees them to move on and cover more ground. Similarly, if someone else says "I got it" to you when you're explaining a point, stop. Ignoring such feedback is a mistake, one that detail-oriented people are particularly vulnerable to. Because they value the details, they feel that others will, too. Of course, not everyone does.

I witnessed how costly this mistake can be in a recent planning session. The project manager continued answering a question long after the man who had asked it said, "I got it." Even when he repeated, "I got it," she calmly and insistently continued. As I watched him get angrier and angrier, I realized she had lost him.

If you're not sure if someone got your point, listen carefully to the person's responses. If it's clear there's still a misunderstanding, suggest "I'm not sure we're on the same page. Let's make sure we understand each other." If the other person gets it, continue with your next point.

Be cognizant of the nonverbal cues that the other person offers. Is he or she growing impatient—nodding, looking away, shifting from side to side? These signals tell you whether or not you still have the listener's attention. If you don't, summarize your point quickly—and move on.

5. The first twenty minutes.

You would never see an NBA all-star casually toss a ball into the air and hope it hits the net. Before each jump shot, players pause, find their footing, set their sights on the net, and visualize a swoosh before the ball has even left their fingertips. You can take the same approach at work by visualizing a successful day before it officially begins. It all comes down to the first twenty minutes.

As soon as you get to work, before you turn on your e-mail or check your voice mail, take twenty minutes to plan the day ahead:

* Define your top priority for the day—the one that you would sacrifice all others to achieve—to help focus your energy.

- Update your "To Do" list. Allot time for everything you need to accomplish, including time to prepare for meetings and other conversations.

- Review your calendar. Determine the purpose of each meeting and appointment. If you don't have one yet, think of one. If you can't determine one, cancel.

- Consider whom you will see in meetings or other events throughout the day. Jot down any issues you need to address with them.

- Glance at your schedule for the remainder of the week and month to make sure you're still focused on the right things.

Then check your e-mail and voice mail and start your day.

6. You're killing me.

What do you do if you've said "I got it" to the person addressing you and they keep right on talking? You feel trapped. You know the clock is ticking. This is the third time you've heard the story. Everyone in the room is already in what I call "violent agreement." Instead of getting angry or giving up, look at the other person, laugh, and say, "You're killing me. I've got the point. Let's move on."

By being both direct and funny about it, you do two things: (1) you break the tension that everyone probably feels; and (2) by keeping things light, you move the conversation forward without offending. Odds are that the speaker is so wrapped up in the point being made that he or she has stopped observing what was going on around them. You're offering him or her a graceful way out and helping to keep things moving.

If you're not comfortable saying "You're killing me," try "Time out." Ask a leading question to direct the conversation in a new direction. Or even suggest a brief break. The point is, find a phrase or method that works for you. If you simply put up with needless repetition, everyone in the room suffers.

7. Get over it.

When someone cuts you off when you're driving, you may feel a surge of anger. Such anger can turn into road rage, fast. The first bump of adrenaline is a healthy response to a threat. It gives you the energy you need to respond promptly and protect yourself—in this case, by slamming on the brakes. But road rage is anything but a healthy reaction. When someone "cuts you off" at work, acknowledge it to yourself, then let it go. Holding on to anger costs time, energy, and focus. If you feel yourself slipping into "office rage":

- Don't take any precipitous action until you've calmed down.
- Take a walk, or talk behind closed doors with someone you trust so that you can let off a little steam.

Don't let your anger cause you to take action in a way that you will regret later.

* Make sure you do not take out your anger in other ways. If you're upset that a colleague was promoted over you, don't allow it to affect your relationship with everyone around you.

* Let your anger go. You cannot change the past. Learn what you can from it and move on.

In some cases, it's important to confront a situation that makes you angry. Did your colleague really do something wrong? Respectfully challenging a new proposal that you presented is his or her right. If, however, he or she ridiculed your ideas rather than constructively responded to them, meet with this person one-on-one. Tell him or her how their action affected you, and ask that it not happen again. Then put it behind you.

Anger steals time and energy. Reacting inappropriately when you are angry makes it even worse and can undermine your career. Just move on.

8. It's not always about you.

When my colleague recently arrived for a sales call with the CEO of one of the world's largest ad agencies, the CEO met him at the elevator, looking rushed and preoccupied. He said, "I only have fifteen minutes." Many people would have instantly deflated, thinking, "He doesn't really want to talk to me—I might as well give up right now." Instead, my colleague said, "No problem. We're prepared—we'll move fast." The CEO's mood instantly brightened. They had a great meeting that did, in fact, end in less than fifteen minutes. My colleague was smart enough to realize that the CEO's mood had nothing to do with him. Because of that he was able to stay focused and on point.

Whether you're dealing with a boss, colleague, client, customer, or spouse, the other person's mood often has nothing to do with you. As human beings we tend to think the other person's mood reflects something we did or didn't do—that it's all about us. Or, as a friend of mine puts it, "We're all the stars of our own movies." But putting ourselves in the center of every situation can distract us unnecessarily. We waste time wondering what we did wrong or how we can fix someone else's issue, when it's not necessarily our fault or concern. Don't.

If you're genuinely concerned that you've offended someone without realizing it, ask them. If the person tells you it has nothing to do with you, offer your support. Give your friend or colleague the space needed to deal with whatever is bothering him or her.

Everyone has a bad-hair day every now and then. It's not always about you, so don't assume it is.

9. What's keeping you up at night?

When I consult with executives, I often ask them, "What's keeping you up at night?" This question gets right to the heart of the issues that are critical to their businesses and their careers.

One client answered, "I just want to know what's really going on in my business." His straightforward answer made it clear to us both that he needed to turn his anxiety into action. We built a plan to improve communication and set up a performance dashboard that would regularly give him the vital information about how his company was performing. Another client, whose company had just made a major error that put its customers at risk, replied, "I'm haunted by the thought that it could happen again. People are counting on me to make sure that it never will." In this instance, we decided to do a formal process review, install new communication hardware throughout the facility, and increase training. Both actions resulted from a practical—yet fundamental—decision: Listen to your deepest concerns and convert them into practical solutions.

Leave a pen and paper by your bed. When the issues of the day start to nag at you, make a note. The payoff is immediate. Writing down your worries will actually help you let go of them so you can sleep. Then take those pages with you to work. As you prepare for the day, look them over and sketch out how you can alleviate your concern. They could be as far-reaching as building an enterprise-wide performance dashboard or as simple as scheduling time to have an uncomfortable, but necessary, conversation you've been avoiding with a colleague. The key is to identify the issue and determine how you will address it. Create a time frame for carrying out your plan. Hold yourself to it.

Not only will you work more effectively, you'll sleep better, too.

10. Don't hide your passion.

When I sense your enthusiasm for your work, you've got me. I'm not talking about empty boosterism. I'm referring to the clear thinking and will-to-win focus that makes others want to share your enthusiasm. When people perform their work with this kind of passion, I want to cheer.

A manager I know once hired an administrative assistant who was so enthusiastic about her job, so eager to learn and excited about the work at the firm, that he invested time and financial resources to help her to grow into new roles. Her passion let him know that it was an investment worth making. And he was right—she's now an executive herself. And she continues to tear into every new task given her. As I see it, her future is unlimited.

My point? Don't be afraid to show excitement for what you do. Too often people try to appear above the fray by staying emotionally aloof. Believe me, it doesn't work. If you're looking to stir others to action—from returning your phone calls to getting your project approved—get them excited about what you're doing. You'll see surprising results.

Think Clearly

11. Start with the end in mind.

Know what you want to achieve *before* you start. Defining the purpose of meetings, projects, and conversations will not only keep you on target, it will also make you more agile when handling bumps in the road. Nothing helps you to move forward like a clear vision of what you want to achieve in the end.

Years ago, a friend told me that he really didn't know where he was headed in his career. "Close your eyes and picture where you want to be and where you want your family to be in five years," I told him. Together, using a flip chart, we set a course for him to achieve his goals. That exercise and discussion had a profound influence on his life and career.

- Whenever you make an appointment or jot down a reminder about an assignment, add a note about why it's important. Review these at the beginning of each day.

* Begin each meeting and project by letting everyone know what you want to achieve. The clearer you are about your objectives, the more likely people will work to help you accomplish them.

End each day by scanning your objectives to see how many you have met. You will probably not have achieved everything you set out to do. That's life. But commit to three things: (1) know the purpose of everything you do, (2) let others know exactly what you want to achieve, and (3) stay focused on your goals. You will be surprised at how often you'll achieve them.

12. Focus on one thing at a time.

Multitasking is overrated. When you're going back and forth between complicated projects, it is impossible to focus properly on each one. Researchers call this "task switching," an action that, itself, requires time and energy. Depending on how many tasks you are juggling, you could be losing 20 to 40 percent of your time, because you have to reengage your focus and thoughts.*

Both life and work require a certain amount of juggling. Few days play out in an orderly, linear sequence. Speaking on the phone to a client or colleague while you're reading a report or typing an e-mail might not cost you that much.

* "Executive Control of Cognitive Processes in Task Switching," Joshua S. Rubinstein, U.S. Federal Aviation Administration, Atlantic City, NJ; David E. Meyer and Jeffrey E. Evans, University of Michigan, Ann Arbor, MI, *Journal of Experimental Psychology—Human Perception and Performance*, Vol. 27, No. 4.

But doing so while you're preparing a report for your department might. At the very least, it will slow you down and result in subpar work.

To increase your focus and performance when concentration is critical, cut down on the multitasking addiction.

- Turn off your e-mail alarm. (Who needs to be alerted to spam?) Check it regularly when it's convenient for *you*—not when it interrupts you.
- Block out time for projects that require intense focus, such as writing, drafting a presentation, or conducting analysis. Forward your calls to voice mail and close your door if necessary. Let people know that you're working on a project. If you don't have a door, put up a sign.
- When possible, schedule important phone conversations when you know you'll have no distractions. Never work on something else while you're on the phone. The person on the other end knows when you're writing an e-mail while you talk, and it's probably irritating him or her.

Organize your work so that you can do one thing at a time and do it well. The payoff will be substantial.

13. Organize yourself *first*.

A professional kitchen is a hot, cramped place full of people working under tremendous time constraints. Chefs don't have the option of coming in on the weekend to catch up. In fact, the weekends are already their busiest times. When the doors to the restaurant open, the race begins. In an industry with notoriously slim profit margins, chefs must turn out an extraordinary number of high-quality meals fast, with the least possible waste. How do they do it?

They get organized *first*. The phrase they use to describe their workspace is "mise en place," a French phrase that means "put in place" (or, more loosely, "everything in its place"). *Before* a chef begins cooking, he or she must anticipate all the equipment and food he or she will need and have them at arm's reach. A chef always places things in the same order and space, as if they were an extension of his or her body. In restaurants, this kind of organization defines the difference between success and failure.

You should do the same in your workspace. Get organized *before* you do anything else. Don't waste time looking for things—whether on your desk or on your computer. Put them where you can find them quickly. Set up systems for organizing your day, your staff, your equipment and supplies, your information and thoughts.

Once you find a place for everything, stick to your system. Eventually, knowing where things belong will become second nature. You'll never have to waste time searching for a file, an e-mail, or a document again.

14. Assumptions kill.

A young entrepreneur had just gotten a big break—a feature article touting his company's products in an influential trade magazine that promised to reach 30,000 potential customers. The article came out and, as expected, the writer raved about the products. Unfortunately, the Web address the journalist included was wrong. The entrepreneur had considered sending the journalist the correct Web site, but assumed that he had seen it in her e-mail signature. Of course, the journalist hadn't seen it and instead got the e-mail address from an old vendor. The result: thousands of missed potential sales.

Don't assume people around you understand what you want. Don't assume your boss knows what you are spending your time on. Don't assume that conditions will be the same next year as they were this year. If you hear someone saying, "I'm sure they know" or "They *must* understand that," put on the brakes immediately. Such verbal signals indicate that you or the other person are not sure of the answer. If it's important enough to do, then take the time to be sure it gets done.

15. Think in bullets.

We all love bullets.

* They add punch to a presentation.
* They're easy to read.
* They get right to the point.

But where are those bullets when you're having a conversation, a one-on-one meeting, or a business lunch? Every professional interaction demands focused, succinct communication. But how do you speak with the same kind of precision that bullets bring to the page?

The secret is clear thinking. Whenever you're involved in any kind of business conversation, take notes. Start by jotting down what you want to achieve and what you think the other person wants. Then listen carefully. Take notes of what's being said and your responses. Doing so allows you to listen thoughtfully. It frees you from trying to keep track of each thought. It also helps you organize your thoughts into bullets. Ask questions if you need clarification.

Before you speak, take a moment to consider what you really want to say. Convey it in clear, distinct bites of information. Lots of bright professionals "think out loud"— that's great for discussions intended to generate new ideas. But when your conversation has a set agenda, or when you're looking to reach conclusions and define a course of action, processing thoughts aloud distracts and confuses others.

If you have content-rich comments to share, take the time to lay them out carefully. Make sure you are connecting with your colleague.

Thinking in bullets doesn't mean firing off points like a semiautomatic weapon, giving your companion no chance to shoot back. It means conveying your purpose clearly, eliminating extraneous commentary, and opening up a purposeful dialogue.

16. Trust your gut.

Jesse, a VP of a small business unit, knew something wasn't right. An account manager had reported that a client, frustrated by the firm's billing practices, wasn't planning to renew her contract. It just didn't add up for Jesse—they'd never had any problems with billing before. He couldn't shake the feeling in his gut that something else was wrong.

Jesse decided to request a one-on-one meeting with the client. When they met, he saw that she was, as reported, frustrated with the firm's billing practices. But he was surprised to learn that, contrary to the account manager's report, she was not planning to terminate the account. Jesse quickly realized that the source of the problem was the account manager. He'd purposely been casting the company in a poor light. Digging a little deeper, Jesse learned that the account manager was planning to start his own company and had been laying the groundwork to take this client with him. Jesse took the steps necessary to protect his client relationships by moving the account manager out.

For decades, credible research has been mounting to pull "intuition" out of the field of the paranormal and place it squarely in the arena of scientific understanding. Researchers know now that our brains are continuously taking in and storing away information, often when we're not even paying attention. And as you gain new experiences, your decision-making abilities improve. Your brain becomes incredibly effective at sorting this raw heap of information into patterns and storing it away until you need it. (As one CEO put it, "The more data and experience I have, the better my intuition gets.")

So when you have a strong gut feeling about a person, issue, or concern, listen to yourself. If you have the time, try to analyze what is making you feel uncomfortable (or comfortable). When you *don't* have the time to dissect your reaction, trust your gut.

17. Predict how long things will take.

You can't control time. But you *can* control how you plan and budget time by accurately predicting how long things take.

When I first started reviewing materials in preparation for quarterly board meetings, I gave myself one hour. It took me only one or two meetings to realize that I needed to schedule at least five hours if I was going to really contribute. On the other hand, I used to budget ninety minutes to help a client develop his board's agenda. Today we need only a half hour. In both cases, my ability to schedule time effectively in the future depends on understanding how long things take.

As you review your "To Do" list this week, make a note about how much time you think each task is going to take. When you complete the task, note how long it actually took. Include interruptions. They're inevitable, so you need to budget time for them. Don't try to work faster yet. Just observe. Do this for several weeks.

Next, review the difference between your estimated and actual time for each task. Did you tend to overestimate the time needed, or were you consistently under? Do you consistently fall behind on days full of meetings? Do you overestimate how long difficult tasks will take and put them off? Look for patterns. The next time you're scheduling your time, increase or decrease your estimations accordingly, based on what you've learned. Continue this exercise until your estimations match reality.

Knowing how long things take is a skill that will help you take control of your day and your life. Moreover, your colleagues and your team will appreciate your ability to set realistic goals—and meet them.

18. Tailor your message to your audience.

Don't be so focused on your message that you lose sight of whom you are addressing. Every communication will be more effective and on point if you spend time considering your audience. And it will take you less time to prepare.

Recently, a CEO held a meeting with every employee in his small company to tell them that the board of directors had sold the company. Before going in, he thought carefully about how the news would affect all 100 people in the room. He knew that many of them would be afraid for their jobs and all of them would be apprehensive about the change to come. Even though the case to sell the organization was strong—in fact, selling it was the only logical choice—he knew that most of the line staff was not familiar enough with the underlying business realities to understand the situation. He decided to be direct and completely forthcoming. He began by announcing the sale. He reassured them that their jobs were safe and talked as openly as he could about timing and integration, the very first questions to come to everyone's mind. Then he gave a short rationale for the sale and told them what they needed to do to help with the transition. He kept his message short but offered to stay and take questions afterward. Despite the fact that the news was hard for many to hear, and some had a number of challenging questions, the presentation went well. Why? Because he was completely focused on his audience. On the other hand, if he'd gone in and presented the information as if he were talking to the local business media, he'd have fallen flat on his face. His company would likely have come to a standstill in terms of productivity.

Whether you're writing a report, a letter, or a presentation, ask yourself:

1) Who's the audience?
2) What are they looking for?
3) How much detail do they want or need?
4) How will the information I have help them in going forward?
5) How much background information do they need?
6) Is anyone likely to be hostile toward what I have to say?
7) Are they familiar with industry jargon?

8) What kinds of examples and analogies will be most helpful to them?

You can't cut to the chase unless you know to whom you are talking.

19. What's been going better lately—
and why?

People usually take the time to analyze their mistakes so they can avoid them in the future. But it's equally important to understand your *triumphs* so you can repeat them without wasting time going back to the drawing board. By studying your successes—whether a specific project, last quarter's sales, or general team performance—you stand a better chance of repeating that success.

One organization increased their sales by 200 percent in one year. But they failed to ask what was behind their phenomenal growth. They reasoned that as long as they didn't change anything, their growth would continue. They even staffed up to deliver on all the new business they anticipated. The next year, however, sales fell off dramatically. This time they looked hard at the previous year's performance to better understand it. They saw that a significant percentage of their growth had been driven by one account manager's relationship with a single client. Toward the end of the year the manager, who normally excelled at staying in touch and anticipating the client's needs, had gotten distracted by personal issues. No one at the firm was maintaining the relationship. Another company seized the opportunity to start building a relationship with the client, drawing off business. If the first company had analyzed the reasons behind their successful year, they'd have ensured that the relationship was being protected. Instead, they had to expend a tremendous amount of energy the following year just to break even. There are two valuable lessons here: (1) the importance of managing relationships—after all, it's easier to keep an existing client happy than chase after a new one; and (2) the realization of how crucial it is to analyze success so that you can repeat it.

Take the time to understand what's behind your success. It's the best way to ensure it will continue.

Speed Up

20. Explode out of the blocks.

Most sprinters will tell you that a good start is half the race. Positioning yourself to explode out of the blocks will help you to build momentum and set yourself up for a winning race.

Similarly, starting the morning off right each day will help you explode out of the blocks at work and maintain that pace all day. Before you step foot in your office, do something to energize yourself. Get up twenty to thirty minutes earlier if you have to. Build in the time to start your engine. Otherwise, you run the risk of arriving at the office each day complaining of low energy and morale. By doing something for yourself *before* you do anything else, you'll feel better all day long.

Eat a healthy breakfast, stretch, walk, exercise—all are good ways to explode out of the blocks. As soon as I stepped out of the shower, I used to pick up my Black-Berry to check e-mails. With no time to eat, I'd grab a but-tered roll on my way to work. By late morning, my energy was zapped. Only when I started taking a few extra min-utes to have a healthy breakfast did my entire day change. Not only did I perform with more energy, but starting the day by first taking care of myself improved my whole out-look. I instantly began dealing more effectively with prob-lems and distractions and getting more done.

Decide what will help *you* explode into the day and sus-tain your energy for the long haul.

21. Every second counts.

There are only so many seconds in a week, and every one of them matters. But how you use them is up to you. Decide what you will do with your career and your life. Don't let it just happen to you.

To better appreciate and use the limited time you have, set aside an hour over the weekend and find someplace to work quietly. Write down this question: What is the purpose of my life? Then start taking notes. Your answer may arise quickly or take some time. But don't give up until you've come up with several sentences that describe your life's purpose. Next, ask yourself how each part of your life—work, friends, family, hobbies—aligns with or relates to that purpose. Again, write it down. Are you spending your time on the things that will help you achieve your purpose? If not, you know you have to make some changes. When your actions are at odds with your goals, you need to take appropriate steps.

This may seem like a simple exercise, but few people do it. The truth is you probably already know your purpose and goals. But you may have pushed them off to the side. Or you may not have aligned your daily actions with your long-term goals. Doing this exercise will help you to do so. A few minutes of quiet reflection can give your life the clarity and sense of purpose you lack.

To keep your day-to-day choices in sync with your life's purpose, take a moment to consider your purpose before you make any major decisions or take on any new responsibilities. It will help you remember the precious importance of every second.

22. Know how things really get done.

My firm was called in to work with an organization that was struggling to integrate a newly acquired company into their own. We interviewed managers from both companies to get a sense of what was going on. The problem became clear. Although the acquiring company worked through short e-mails or a casual encounter at a colleague's desk, the newly acquired company was trying to follow the acquirer's *formal* policies and procedures. They were time-consuming processes involving detailed forms and systems. The acquiring company's employees had long ago figured out how to work around them. But the new employees didn't know any better. So they were constantly getting bogged down in red tape. In this case, we helped the acquiring company streamline their processes. But the takeaway lesson is that the way you get things done in theory is often not the way things actually get done on a practical level.

If you find yourself getting frustrated over how long a task is taking, find out who the right person is to speed the process along. Often, the people who grease the skids of an organization aren't part of the formal reporting hierarchy. Knowing whom to go to, and learning how things really get done, is vital in any organization.

23. Build momentum.

When someone tells you they're "on a roll," that's momentum. When a basketball team scores every time they go down the court and forces three turnovers in a row, that's momentum. When you're consistently beating deadlines on a project, that, too, is momentum. While it's relatively easy to build momentum on small tasks, it is also possible to build momentum on big, time-consuming projects. And, as the laws of physics tell us, the payoff is even greater.

Anyone who has ever tried to keep a large group on task throughout a long project knows that it's challenging. The more people involved and the longer the timeline, the more opportunities there are for distractions to slow down the entire group. But a lot of people means a lot of money, so it's all the more critical to stick to a cut to the chase work ethic. The secret is creating momentum.

Here's how an insurance company used momentum to keep a major initiative on course for over two years:

1) *Make momentum part of the plan.* Everyone on the team agreed they wouldn't move ahead until they knew how to create momentum.

2) *Grab the low-hanging fruit.* The team selected three minor "wins" and tackled them before they did anything else. (Look for initiatives that no one will object to, that won't cost much, and that will be fairly easy to carry out.) If you can, choose several of these. Then get them done. It sends a signal to the entire team that you are on the move.

3) *Go for* one *big win.* A company I've worked with committed to changing the culture of the most resistant part of the organization. It was an audacious move, but a crucial one. The energy from the early wins helped them get it done. A lot of companies fall into the trap of trying to do too much at once. This group recognized that in order to achieve and sustain momentum, they needed to choose one important thing and really deliver on it.

4) *Celebrate the early successes publicly.* As soon as they started seeing real results, they celebrated. They sent e-mails congratulating everyone on the team and copied their bosses. They gave updates at staff meetings and praised the people involved.

By measuring and communicating success throughout the project, the firm was able to keep building momentum. The energy kept a team of fourteen people from ten departments with competing priorities engaged for the long haul and delivered great results for everyone involved.

24. Make sure your handoffs are clean.

Many relay races are lost in the handoff. When a baton is dropped, it's almost impossible to regain the lost time. Scheduling a project that involves several people creates a similar challenge—one that demands coordination and concentration. You can manage this risk by defining the handoffs, responsibilities, and deadlines from the start.

Start by meeting with your team and writing down the project's objective. Then list the tasks necessary to achieving that goal. Next to each task, write a conservative estimate of how many days or weeks the task will require. Then draw a line between the related tasks. These are your handoffs. For example, if the research department is studying what images will work best on a marketing brochure and the design department is laying out the brochure, a handoff will be necessary. Assign a date to each handoff and you've got a battle plan. Make sure everyone on the team has a copy so they are ready to take over when the project reaches them.

Relay races are rife with dropped batons—but your projects don't have to be. Mapping handoffs ahead of time ensures that no one misses a step.

25. Bag consensus.

When you're working on a project, it's important to get input from the key players involved. But you can't afford to sit around and wait for everyone to agree. Decide how you're going to make a final decision *before* asking for input.

One executive was so addicted to getting agreement from everyone that when faced with the challenge of integrating another company into his own, he held meeting after meeting to make sure that *everyone* was enthusiastic about his strategy. By the time he was ready to implement his strategy, it was too late—the acquired company had begun to implode. It ruined his career.

When you ask people for input, let them know up front when and how your decision will be made. That way, if they miss the deadline, you're not obligated to slow down.

Whenever possible, appoint one person the final decision maker. Whether it's you or someone you've chosen, the final decision maker is ultimately accountable for the project's success.

When you're part of a team working on a project with a large scope, different people may be responsible for different decisions. Again, this does *not* mean you need to struggle for unanimity. Get input from the key people involved in the project, as well as anyone else whose insight or knowledge can help you get a better result. Then discuss their input, make decisions, and move.

Complete consensus is often impossible—don't waste time waiting for everyone to agree. Before asking anyone for their input, decide how to decide.

26. Break through silos.

Silos are a colossal waste of time and energy. Break them down by opening up lines of communication.

Take a cue from Mike Bloomberg, a master at getting results. When he set up the Bloomberg L.P. offices, he deliberately had the space designed so that employees would regularly bump into each other. Every employee enters through the fifteenth-floor reception area, where they gain access to other floors via a spiral staircase that's always filled with people moving from one place to another. Employees are encouraged to interact with colleagues in the large, centrally located snack bars that are well stocked with complimentary food. To further demonstrate his belief in the electricity of ideas, instead of an office, Bloomberg simply set up a desk for himself in one corner of the Bloomberg broadcast newsroom.

When Bloomberg moved to New York's City Hall as mayor, he brought with him the belief that people function best when they communicate eye to eye. He blew away the generations-old tradition that honored city execs with large private offices that separated them from their staffs. Now they sit in cubicles—as does he—in a large open space. A Bloomberg workplace practically pulses with the vitality of face-to-face contact. And it pays off. Communication is excellent. Energy and accountability are high.

Build this kind of dynamic with your own team or office. Create a workspace and culture that encourages teamwork. Reward employees for building strong working relationships across departmental lines. Encourage them to share information freely with colleagues in other areas. And practice what you preach.

You don't need to be the CEO or even a department head to break down silos. Make it a point to build relationships—both formal and informal—with colleagues throughout your organization. Ask for short one-on-one meetings to learn more about their goals and projects. Invite them to join a cross-departmental team if they have the time. If they don't, offer to brief them regularly on the relevant aspects of your work.

Breaking down silos will help you and your company get more done. In the process, you'll be building relationships that will help drive your career forward. Such openness pays off on every level.

27. Appeal to their enlightened self-interest.

Which television ad would catch your attention? A breakfast cereal "loaded with fiber and vitamins" or one that will "lower your blood pressure and cholesterol level and help prevent a stroke"? I'll bet it's the second approach, because it appeals to your "enlightened self-interest."

When you're trying to sell something—be it a product, a service, even an idea—don't just tell them about it. Tell people how it will benefit their lives. When you ask for support from the people around you, don't just say, "I need this done by the end of the week." Instead, explain why staying on target now will lead to accolades for the entire team in terms of their careers, bonuses—even promotions.

Here are a few examples of information on features that have been "repackaged" to appeal to one's enlightened self-interest:

Features	Benefits
This car has antilock breaks and a passenger-side airbag.	This car will save your life. (An excellent example is the "Volvo saved my life club"—www.volvocars.com.)
We will prepare your taxes and send them to you, ready to sign.	Our customer's tax refunds are 25 percent higher than the average.
You'll be working as part of a cross-departmental team.	You'll be increasing your visibility in the company and working with people who can jump-start your career.
The speaker you're considering for your conference specializes in leadership.	The last CEO who hired the speaker said, "He made me look like a hero and inspired my people to raise our profits by 80 percent."

Getting cooperation from other people can consume a major part of your day. Show others how your plan serves their own interests. You cut to the chase on two levels. You'll get their commitment faster, and that commitment will help you get more done.

28. Measure twice, cut once.

This old carpenter's adage isn't just about saving resources. It's also about saving time. Once a piece of wood is cut to the wrong length, it's hard to find another use for it. But it's *impossible* to regain the lost time. And the more valuable the materials and time-consuming the process, the more important it is to get it right the first time.

You measure and "cut" into your resources every day—your time, your team or company's time, your money, your technological capacity. So getting it right the first time is critical. Before committing yourself or your group to a course of action, analyze the costs and benefits. If you're recommending a new product or service, research the impact it will have on other people, your company, department, or group. If you're planning to send someone from your team to participate on a cross-departmental project, make sure you're sending the right person for the job.

In each case, by "measuring twice"—by making sure you've gotten all the information you need before you spend resources—you'll actually save time and money.

29. Close the loop.

Have you ever had a test at your physician's office, and the nurse said, "We'll call you if there's a problem"? Two weeks later—and still no call. You begin to wonder, "What if they lost the blood sample? How can I be sure everything's okay?"

When people don't close the loop, they leave the other person hanging. Not only is it distracting, it can subtly erode the relationship.

Anyone can follow up. It's a simple matter of being conscientious and disciplined.

- When a colleague introduces you to a new contact, tell your colleague when you've reached out to the new person. After you've connected, tell your colleague how it went.

- Respond to invitations and meeting requests promptly. It's a lot easier for others to plan an event when they know who's coming.
- When you receive details or specifics, acknowledge them. When you receive a question by phone or e-mail, answer it or forward it to the person who can. Acknowledge your action with the person who raised the question. A simple e-mail reply saying, "Got your message, see you there" will eliminate any confusion or uncertainty over whether you received the e-mail and were able to attend the event.

Never let yourself be known as someone who leaves other people hanging. Once that label gets applied, it's hard to shake. On the other hand, when you consistently close the loop, you build a reputation as a dependable professional.

Make a habit of closing the loop in everything you do. Tell the people you work with to do the same.

30. Call an audible.

In football, when the defense sets up in a way that makes it impossible for the offense to execute their play, the smart quarterback calls an audible to change the play at the line of scrimmage. In a game last season, the Cowboys led the Giants 24–21. With no time-outs left and the clock running down, Giants QB Eli Manning lined up at the Cowboys' nine-yard line, intending to pass. When he saw the Cowboys' safeties playing back in the coverage—anticipating a pass—he changed the passing play he'd called in the huddle to a running play. He faked the throw and handed off to Tiki Barber, who scored the touchdown to win the game.

Frequently in business, in order to gain an edge on the competition, you need to anticipate change *before* it happens—and react immediately. As soon as you sense a shift that could present a new challenge or opportunity—a new competitor, technology that's transforming your industry, even a natural disaster—call an audible for your team. Pay attention to what's happening around you. Communicate regularly with your team about strategy, roles, and expectations. That way, when an opportunity presents itself—and in business, it always will—you can respond immediately.

31. Beat change to the punch.

Carl Jung once said, "If there's a fear of falling, the only safety consists in deliberately jumping." New technologies, a new boss, a new direction for the company—change is coming at you from every direction. Don't wait for it to take you by surprise. Beat change to the punch.

I recently saw how resistance to change devastated the careers of two men I know. When their companies merged, the two men, who were regional vice presidents, were asked to collaborate on an integration strategy. They fought on every aspect of the integration until the CEO put them in the same room and said, "What are you going to tell your families when I have to fire you both?" Sadly, neither could move forward and both were eventually fired. Had they used the project as an opportunity to show their worth to the new enterprise, both would be flourishing in high-level jobs today.

The next time change is staring you in the face, decide to make the most of the new situation, whatever it is:

- If your company has been bought, learn all you can about the acquiring company. Think creatively about new opportunities the acquisition creates. Then draft a one-page memo to share your thinking with your boss.
- If you're working for a new boss, e-mail your congratulations and request a meeting. Ask about his or her priorities. Review what you're working on, and offer to help in challenging areas.
- Scan trade publications and talk with peers to discover new technologies, business practices, or processes that might help you do your job better. Talk with your boss about adopting them.

Resisting change wastes time, can burn you out, and causes others to lose patience. Instead, view change as an opportunity. Before long, you won't just respond to change. You'll start seeking it out.

32. To speed up, slow down.

One of the music world's foremost manufacturers of reeds, drumheads, strings, and other accessories—their client list looks like a Who's Who of musicians—recently evaluated their multistep reed-manufacturing process. The hands-on CEO learned that if they slowed down the cutting process by 20 percent, the reeds would be more cleanly severed—so much so that they didn't need polishing after being cut. This discovery eliminated an entire manufacturing step. The time and cost savings of cutting out both the step and the maintenance of the related equipment more than offset the cost of the slower process.

Look for signs that you're moving too fast and creating unnecessary follow-up work. In the coming week, make a note every time you circle back to fix something or get tripped up by moving ahead without a clear purpose.

Look over your "To Do" list for the week. Highlight anything that looks like a redo—they represent a tremendous opportunity to save time. Take care to get them right next time—and every time.

Be Direct

33. Teach people how to use your time.

You can't make the best use of your time unless those around you cooperate. Tell your team exactly how you expect them to use their time—and yours. It doesn't matter how high up in the organization you are. You have a right to help your colleagues make the best use of your time.

Start with your team. Build a culture around effective use of time—both their own and their colleagues'. Tell them exactly how you want them to communicate, prepare for meetings, and present information. Insist on clarity and brevity. Set personal boundaries, such as "If you'd like me to review a substantial document, I'll need forty-eight hours."

Then follow through *consistently*. If you've asked for every meeting to have an agenda, give your team permission to walk out of any meeting without one. If you've requested an executive summary for documents over six pages and you get a ten-page document without one, return it without reading it. Let your team know you're serious and they'll respect your guidelines. Thank them publicly when they do.

Over time, these standards—whether you write them out or convey them informally—will make your team stronger and save you all time.

34. Treat others' time
as you would your own.

Think of this as the Golden Rule to Cutting to the Chase. When you ask for someone else's time, treat it with respect. Others will thank you for it, and you'll stand a better chance of getting the same respect in return. The secret? Prepare for each meeting with your colleagues as if you were preparing for a meeting with the CEO.

And if your meeting is actually *with* the CEO, prepare twice as hard. A CEO was recently invited to go on a sales call by his senior sales executive. After an early-morning flight to Syracuse, New York, in 20-below temperatures, the CEO asked for a briefing: "Tell me what you've got." The sales executive responded with some basics that he'd already shared. The CEO countered, "No, no. I mean, how big is the organization? What's their financial performance? What's their competitive position in the marketplace? What's the relationship to the parent company? Who is the decision maker? What's your agenda?" The sales executive tried to respond, but it was clear that he didn't have valid answers to these key questions. The CEO was furious. Without this information, he would be proceeding at an enormous and potentially embarrassing disadvantage. He'd basically blown an entire day.

Before you ask anyone else to be involved in a conference call or meeting, join a team project, or go on a business trip, think. The first question you need to answer is "Do I really need this person's time? Can I do it on my own?" If you need the other person, define specifically what you need. Explain why their involvement is important. Give them everything they will need to get up to speed.

People don't mind giving their time if they feel it's valued and helpful. It's your responsibility to have thought that through before you approach them.

35. Know what's being asked of you.

Before you start a project, be sure you know exactly what's expected. It's an enormous waste of time to move forward without a clear sense of where you're headed.

Imagine this. Your boss asks you to summarize trends—economic or otherwise—that might affect your organization's success on a prospective project. And she needs it in two days. You conduct the research and analysis, and create a twenty-page document with charts, graphs, and reams of data. You bring it to your boss. She says, "This is great, but I was looking for a one- or two-pager. I need to share it with my boss. He'll never have the patience for this." When she asks you to rewrite it and cut it down to two pages, you're so angry that you waste even more time fuming about it.

The fact is, this is avoidable. When you get an assignment, ask your boss to describe exactly what he or she is looking for. Ask about length, the level of detail, and the deadline. Make sure you're on the same page. Ask for clarification if you don't understand something. Then summarize your understanding of the assignment in an e-mail (include the deadline) and ask your boss to confirm that you've gotten everything right. He or she will applaud you for your foresight in getting things right from the start.

36. If you want something, ask for it.

If you need something, don't beat around the bush. Don't assume people will know what you need, either. Don't make them guess. The more specific you are about what you need, the faster you'll get it.

One executive got in the habit of copying his boss on everything. He assumed that his boss would let him know if there were any problems. Of course, his boss was busy and read only material flagged as requiring approval. When the executive sent his boss the mission statement for his business unit as an attachment, without any indication that he was seeking approval of it, it made its way to the boss's trash bin. Months later, his boss was shocked when the executive handed it out at a meeting. He had a number of changes that could have been made long before and saved the executive embarrassment if the executive had simply asked for his approval.

These four guidelines will help you cut to the chase when asking for what you need:

- If you're asking for something from an employee or peer, clearly frame your request and set a deadline.
- If you're asking for input from your boss on a project, break it into pieces. Ask her what she likes (or doesn't like) about each part of your plan or approach.
- If you need clarification about criticism you've received, ask for specific concerns in as much detail as possible.
- If you want to be kept in the loop, ask to be added to a distribution list or to attend a meeting. Be sure to know what's expected of you in return.
- If you need more resources, explain what you need—and why.

Notice how specific each request is. Such clarity will help ensure that both you and your team get what you need, when you need it.

37. Tell them if the baby is ugly.

When I asked a colleague to review my initial outline for this book, he agreed under one condition: "I need to know that I can tell you if the baby is ugly." I told him that not only did I agree, I was counting on him to constructively challenge my thinking.

When someone has a new idea, he or she often loses objectivity. After all, the idea reflects on his or her creativity and quality of thinking. It's hard to tell someone that you don't like an idea. But it's a lot easier to have that discussion *before* you launch a new product or service than *after* your company spends countless hours and dollars to develop it. In fact, the sooner you point out that the baby is ugly, the less time everyone wastes developing a flawed idea. A smart innovator counts on your honest feedback. That's why he or she is asking for it.

If possible, comment on what works about the idea before you offer criticism. It will help the person remain open to your comments and possibly point him or her in a new direction that works. Then, in direct terms, explain what you feel isn't working. Be specific. If the idea doesn't work because you don't see a market for it, say so. If you think he or she is underestimating the cost, don't keep this to yourself. By showing people the specific flaws in their thinking, you will help them see how they could strengthen the idea or save them from wasting time and energy on something that isn't going to work. They'll thank you someday.

38. Cut to the chase without drawing blood.

If you tend to steamroll over colleagues, you alienate those around you. You may think you're cutting to the chase. In fact, you're merely cutting others off.

I once worked with someone who constantly cut people off in his determination to keep meetings on track. When he felt someone went off on a tangent, he would harshly tell them, "Take it off line." His confrontational approach tended to shut the group down. It's unlikely the person who went off topic would contribute for the rest of the meeting. Worse, my colleague, as a result of his harsh style, lost the input of his coworkers. People stopped going the extra mile for him. Without their cooperation and support, it took him much longer to get things done. His attempt to save time backfired.

Of course, you often *do* have to speak up to keep others

on track. The next time you see a conversation heading off course, remind the group that you have only a limited amount of time together. Ask if you can get back to the main issue (and return to their issue another time). Remember to thank the person when he or she agrees.

You don't need to berate colleagues who digress. Respectfully ask people to stay on point, and they usually will. After all, they don't want to waste time either.

39. Make sure everyone has the map.

Imagine you and some friends are driving to the same destination in different cars. If your friends don't have directions, then they would need to follow you. That can waste a lot of time. Each stoplight slows down the entire caravan. And both followers and leaders are always a little distracted for fear of getting lost or losing the others. If everyone has a map, on the other hand, it doesn't matter whether or not you get separated. You'll still all end up at the same destination. People are free to make minor course changes along the way—they will still end up in the right place.

Our firm's map has five ultimate "destinations," or "drivers," as I call them: First and foremost is Client Satisfaction. Every Monday morning, no matter where the members of my core team might be—in the office or on the road—we have a regularly scheduled meeting to make sure we're all headed in the right direction. Our consultants keep track of their performance in each of the five drivers and the company meets quarterly to review our progress. Because we talk about these goals so often, even when we're not in the same room and decisions need to be made, our team has the map to guide them. For other companies, their map might be their mission statement or growing their core competencies.

Here are two examples to show how the map can work at a practical level. In the first, a senior consultant gets an SOS call from a client on Sunday afternoon. He sees it come in on his caller ID and knows the number. He can let it go into his voice mail or pick up. Our Client Satisfaction driver tells him "pick up," and he does. In the second, an administrator in the office gets a request from a client for a lunch appointment with me that Friday, but I already have a lunch scheduled with a prospective client. Again, because of the Client Satisfaction driver, he knows that I will probably want to meet the established client and reschedule with the prospect. Instead of telling the client I'm booked, he checks in with me first to make me aware of the request.

At every level, having a map works to guide better business decisions.

40. Tell them what's on the test.

Most students don't waste time studying material they don't think will be on the test. Teachers handle this in one of two ways. They carefully conceal what will be on the test so students study *everything* or they tell the students what will be on the test to help them focus. In business, I suggest you take the second option. Telling people how they will be measured will help them focus on the most important things.

First, make sure you know how performance is measured. If you're unclear how your work supports your organization's strategy, meet with your boss. If you work in the marketing department, the performance measures might be the number of qualified leads your team generates. If you're in customer service, the performance measures might focus on high customer satisfaction scores.

Next, tell your team how they will be measured, both as a group and individually. To reinforce performance, link a portion of their compensation to their performance in these areas. Explain why hitting targets is crucial to the business. Don't focus on more than three. Any more than that will defeat your purpose, dividing their attention too broadly.

When your team is focused on the most important things, they'll be less distracted by low-priority matters and achieve more results with less effort.

41. Know your work style—and theirs.

I like working face-to-face. Even in this age of electronic communication, I like to look people in the eye, read their body language, see their thought process, and let them see mine. And everyone on my team knows it. How? Because I've told them. Knowing one another's work styles helps us plan, improves our working relationships, and minimizes confusion and frustration.

If you don't know how you like to work, start observing yourself. The next time you're "in the zone," make note of the circumstances. Was it a particular time of day? Were you brainstorming with others? Were you working alone? Try re-creating that circumstance and observe whether you experience the same kind of productivity.

Then make it known. For instance, if you like to review materials thoroughly before forming an opinion, tell your boss or your team. If you concentrate best in the morning, block out that time for work that requires intense focus and request afternoon meetings instead.

Next, learn your colleagues' work styles. When you begin working with a new colleague or client, or if you sense tension in an existing relationship, ask the other person, "How do you like to work? I want to make sure I'm giving you all the information and time you need." Often they'll tell you directly. But be prepared to ask a few specific questions:

- How do you prefer to take in information? In written form or having someone present it?
- How far in advance of a discussion would you like materials in order to prepare?
- How much detail do you need?
- Would you like people to give you recommendations up front, or do you like to keep your options open?

Everyone works differently. It's just the way we're wired. Eliminate confusion and frustration by knowing your own work style—and theirs.

42. Clear the air.

When you sense that a colleague is angry or upset with you, clear the air. As tempting as it is to avoid an uncomfortable talk, these situations *never* resolve themselves. Even if the dynamic between you and your colleague drifts back to "normal," the unspoken frustration will affect your relationships, and potentially your work.

Recently, one of my colleague's clients switched consultants "for no reason." I suspected there *was* a reason and encouraged my colleague to reach out. When he did, he learned that his former client was frustrated by how hard it was to reach him. By clearing the air, my colleague not only started the process of rebuilding a connection with his client, but also learned the importance of responding promptly to everyone he deals with.

Before you clear the air, ask *yourself* what might be

wrong. If you know that you did something wrong, apologize immediately. You will be surprised by how quickly you'll both be able to move on. If you don't know what's wrong, ask. Be open and honest in listening to their responses. If you feel wronged, explain how you feel without accusing or blaming. Even if you agree to disagree, you've reestablished trust.

If at all possible, talk face-to-face. If you can't connect in person, have the conversation by phone. When you see your colleague next, shake his or her hand and make sure there is no lingering unease. Make it clear how much you value the relationship.

The fear that you've damaged a relationship will gnaw away at you until you confront it. If you sense something's wrong, clear the air.

43. Cut the bull.

Too many business conversations go nowhere because one person is afraid of offending the other. But there's no excuse for dancing around the issue (and no time for it, either). Cut the bull.

Not long ago, a talented newcomer at an insurance company was asked to lead an initiative. Concerned that her colleagues might resent her new role, this usually articulate young professional tried to downplay her contribution by talking around the issue. When asked about her role, she said, "I am more than happy to contribute. I'm committed to this initiative. While I may not be the best person to lead this project—there are so many others equally, if not more, equipped to handle this kind of responsibility—I'm happy to help with whatever you need." The confusion she created over roles took several meetings to clear up. My point? Say what you mean. Don't sugar-coat it.

Make your point clearly and assertively, without being aggressive. Indirectness erodes trust and can cloud the issue. It wastes time and can hurt your career. When you've got something to say, say it and move on. Even if people don't agree with you, they'll respect you for your honesty and candor.

44. Create a "no loitering" zone.

We all know "lingerers." They're the people who come to your office or workspace and start telling you about their son's soccer game or ask if you watched *American Idol* last night. Make a note every time someone stops by to chat during the day. Estimate how much time they spend in your office. Now multiply that number by 250 business days. That will give you the approximate number of hours you will have lost over the course of a year. To most people, that comes to several weeks a year. Wouldn't you rather spend that time on something more productive? If the answer is yes, turn your workspace into a "no lingering" or "no loitering" zone. Start by posting a sign. (You can download a No Loitering Zone sign from our Web site at www.stuartlevine.com.)

When a colleague drops by and you don't have the time to talk:

- Point to your sign and make a joke of it. Make it clear that you don't have any time to waste.
- Apologize. Explain that your plate is full or that you are on a deadline.
- Ask if he or she would like to get coffee later, when you plan to take a break.

If you let them, others will eat up your time to their own benefit or purpose. Make it clear that your time is valuable. They'll come to respect you, and your time, all the more.

45. You can't please everyone.

I wish every situation was win-win. It would make life easier. But sometimes it's not possible. When someone makes an unreasonable request of you, it's okay to say no. You can't please everyone. Attempting to do so will only waste your time.

When a business owner I know, Betty, was expanding her operation, she chose to partner with a team in another city. Despite their agreement that Betty would retain control of the product, one member of the other team wanted to make some changes to make it more appealing in their marketplace. His requests didn't make sense to her. They weren't part of the agreement. But Betty tried to accommodate them because she didn't want to be seen as obstinate or unreasonable. Finally, after the other team pushed for more changes that she believed were inappropriate, she said no. Betty sent an e-mail to them outlining the issue and her position. The head of the other team called her immediately to apologize. The person pushing the changes had been acting on his own. Everyone else was fine with the original product. Betty, of course, felt relieved. But she also realized that she had wasted weeks trying to satisfy them when she should have just said no.

If you find others asking you to do things that are off strategy, or simply a waste of time, don't be afraid to say no. If you are unclear, discuss it with your boss. Saying no to requests that don't make sense will leave you with more time to work on things that add real value.

Meet Smarter

46. People hate meetings for a reason.

Let's face it. There's no aspect of business more reviled than meetings. People resent having their time wasted by the rambling that often takes over at the average meeting. But meetings can also be a great way to get a lot done in little time. Here are three ways to keep the discussion focused on your objective:

STATE YOUR PURPOSE AND SET A CLEAR END POINT.
Start the meeting by stating your purpose. If people start to ramble, let everyone know how much time you have left. Meetings often run over. In fact, too often people expect them to—so it's not enough to write the end time on the agenda. Reminding everyone of the time frame will keep the conversation on point.

SUMMARIZE THE SITUATION.

If the conversation veers off course, say, "So let me summarize what I think I just heard." Doing so will ensure that everyone's on the same page and will instantly refocus the conversation.

ASK FOR IDEAS.

When you ask others for ideas, you immediately focus them on the work at hand and engage their creativity. This is a great way to encourage their participation and give them a stake in the outcome. Just ask, "So where do we go from here?"

Many people hate meetings, but they don't have to. Keep the discussion on point and people may actually begin to value meetings for the effective tools they can be.

47. Every conversation should have a purpose.

The same executives who'd never think of scheduling a meeting longer than thirty minutes often find their business calls and lunches dragging on long after the goal has been met. Even worse, some find these "informal" meetings getting so sidetracked that nothing gets accomplished. Why? Because they failed to prepare as they would for any other meeting. Successful people, on the other hand, never shoot from the hip. Ask yourself these four questions well in advance of the call, talk, or luncheon.

1) What do I want to accomplish?
2) What do I need from the other person?
3) What information do I want to share with this person?
4) What can I do to add value for this person?

Begin the meeting by clearly stating what you'd like to accomplish. Keep your notes on hand. If the other person adds something, jot it down. Before wrapping up, say, "Let's just check back to make sure we achieved everything we wanted to." Don't pay the bill or hang up until you've discussed what happens next. One exception: If the purpose of your lunch or conversation is to build a relationship, don't formally state your objective. However, make sure you've shared or learned everything you'd hoped to by meeting's end.

Think about how much time you spend on the phone and in "informal" meetings. Making the best use of that time will really pay off.

48. 120 seconds and out.

Many interactions can be handled in the time it takes to read this rule. A quick question, an update, approval over a document—none of these requires a major discussion. But too often people feel rude dropping by another person's office for only a minute or two. Ironically, that's exactly what the person on the other side of the desk is hoping they'll do. For these kinds of exchanges, call ahead. Ask for two minutes. When you arrive, spend no more than two minutes delivering your message.

The other day, I was meeting with an executive when an employee asked for a couple of minutes to discuss a time-sensitive matter. She agreed. The employee came into her office and launched into a to-the-point discussion about a new client: "We agreed to deliver two levels of service to this client within the next two months for a price of $40,000.

To beat the promised delivery date, we'll go over budget by about 10 percent. But this is a new client with tremendous revenue potential, so I'd like to impress them. Are you comfortable with that?" It was a picture-perfect case of cutting to the chase. The employee gave his boss everything she needed to know in order to answer his question. He made a recommendation and closed by asking for her approval. He was out the door in less than a minute with his boss's OK.

Your bosses and your employees will appreciate this kind of brevity and preparedness. Better yet, they'll adopt your style and return the favor.

49. Know when you're not needed.

Before agreeing to participate in any meeting, conference call, or project, ask yourself, do I really need to be involved? Can they get the job done without me? If the answer is yes, take yourself out of the loop.

Recently, I met with a few key executives of a financial institution to prepare for a strategy session being held later that morning. Another member of the larger strategy team, an executive vice president, stopped by and asked, "What time is the meeting?" Told it would be starting in about forty-five minutes, he replied, "Okay; let me know when you need me." I've known any number of people who would have felt the need to join the pre-meeting. The fact that he didn't told me that he was a smart, confident executive who wasn't threatened by discussions taking place without him.

Review your commitments over the next two weeks. Flag those—from conference calls to business trips— where someone else from your company or team will be present. Ask yourself, do I really need to go? If you're on the fence, consider these questions:

- Do I bring a unique perspective or special knowledge to the discussion?
- Will I benefit from being involved?
- Am I concerned that my colleagues will not be able to achieve the objective?

If your answer to these questions was "no," tell those who will be attending that you're sure they can handle it without you. Doing so will free you to focus on your own work—and allow those around you to step up to the plate.

Successful people know when they're not needed—and that's a great way to cut to the chase.

50. Master the ten-minute meeting.

The higher up in an organization you go, the more likely you will see appointments being scheduled in ten-minute slots. Below the top level, half an hour seems to be the shortest meeting achievable. Whenever possible, go for ten.

Think about your last talk with your doctor. It was probably very important—and very brief. Smart patients write down their thoughts and questions in advance to make sure they've covered everything before they leave. If you can have a "meeting" this important in ten minutes, you can do the same at work.

Look through your calendar for the week. Ask yourself, how many of these meetings can be cut to ten minutes? What would you have to do to accomplish your objectives in a third of the time? Make notes about what you need to cover and create a list of any questions you need answered.

When the meeting starts, tell your colleagues, "I think we can actually knock this out in a few minutes if we stay on point." That will get others involved and focused right away. Don't rush through important issues, but keep discussions moving. You'll be surprised how much you can get done in ten minutes.

51. Count noses.

Business is all about getting support—from getting approval of a project to getting additional resources to securing funding for an investment idea. It usually comes down to getting several key people to back your ideas. It might take place in a meeting with a formal vote or as the result of an informal conversation. Whatever form it takes, know who the key players are in getting a decision—and where each of them stands before a decision is made. Otherwise you might find your efforts stymied.

I learned this the hard way when I was a young legislator in Albany, New York. I proposed legislation that would require pharmacists to put a drug's name on the bottle (there was a time when prescriptions came only with instructions) and to post their prices so people could comparison-shop. I was young and inexperienced. I assumed that my arguments would stand on their own against the opposition, who felt the government would be placing an undue time burden on pharmacists. When I lost that legislation by two votes, I was caught completely off guard. My proposal ultimately became law, but I had to fight the entire battle a second time. The lesson I learned? The next time we headed into the legislative chamber, I knew exactly how everyone in that room planned to vote.

Before an official "vote" is held, meet one-on-one with the key people to explain your position. Learn about their concerns. Listen for ways to adapt or modify your proposal to serve their needs as well as yours. Ask them directly, "Will you support me on this product development program?" If they seem uncomfortable giving their endorsement, find out what would make them feel more comfortable with what you're proposing. Work to earn their support so that you can count on it later.

Even if you're not able to win everyone's support, you should at least know where everyone stands. If you have the right people on your side, you will still get what you need the overwhelming majority of the time and you'll have established a closer relationship with the key decision makers in the office. If you don't have enough support to move your idea through, table it. If you are voted down and your standing in the company is weakened, this will make it harder to restate your case or win the next battle. Sometimes cutting to the chase means waiting until the moment is right.

52. Stay on course.

Nothing is more frustrating than reaching the finish line of a project and discovering that somewhere in the journey you took a left instead of a right and lost your way.

The good news is, it is possible to stay on track, even with the most complicated projects, when the stakes are highest. Early in his career, a colleague of mine worked on the fifty-person team that designed and built the lunar landing module—an audacious, complex, resource-intense, long-term project. Every morning, the entire team met for ten minutes to hear project leaders give a two-minute summary of issues to manage that day. By the end of the meeting, everyone was in the loop. Because the team talked regularly, their talks were brief and completely focused.

Schedule regular meetings with your team, division, or department to give and receive updates and make sure all the key players are on the same page. Discuss risks or possible problems, as well as ways to streamline processes so things run as smoothly as possible. Brief the person—your boss or a client, for example—who will be evaluating your success regularly, as well. By keeping everyone on course, you'll hit the finish line a lot faster.

53. Don't grandstand.

We all know someone who likes to hear himself talk. Every meeting is a chance to perform, and no comment goes unquestioned. Don't be this guy. You're wasting everyone's time, including your own.

In fairness, most people who dominate conversations aren't aware of it. They probably enjoy talking or process information by talking about it. If this is your style, however, take a look at the possible consequences. People may be shutting you out, not inviting you to meetings, or failing to give you the support you need.

Next time you're in a meeting, make sure you're really participating as a member of a team. If people turn to you every time there is a lull in the conversation, that's a sign that you may be overdoing it. Concentrate on listening and asking questions. When others turn to you, anticipating that you'll have a comment, say, "I'd like to hear what Joan thinks about this. Joan?" Write your thoughts down and choose the best time to share them. Never cut people off.

Most of us could stand to listen and watch people's faces more and talk less. We'd all get a lot more out of conversations that way.

54. Have a meeting before the meeting.

When you have an important meeting scheduled, you'll need to work in sync with your team in order to cut to the chase. Have a meeting before the meeting to make sure you're on the same page.

Though the length of a pre-meeting will vary depending on what you're trying to achieve, you'll usually need only ten or fifteen minutes. Say, for example, you and a team-mate have been asked to meet with the head of a company that your boss is considering as a major supplier. Two days before you are scheduled to meet, work through this list of questions:

What do we want to achieve?	We want to understand their business and clearly identify the potential benefits and risks to both parties.

What does the other company want to achieve?	They want to do business with us, so they'll be looking for ways to meet our needs. They will also want to understand the process for getting a decision made on our end.
What are each of our responsibilities before and during the meeting?	You will talk with our boss about the decision-making process and draft a meeting agenda. I'll take the lead in the meeting.

Whether you're planning for a meeting with another department, a potential client, or a valued customer, it's essential to make sure you and your team members are on the same page. Keep your pre-meeting short and focused. Think of it as practice for the big game.

55. Debrief.

After every major meeting or presentation, conduct a debrief with your team to discuss how things went. Ask yourselves, "Did we accomplish everything we set out to do? Is everyone clear on the next steps?" Ask if anyone has any suggestions about what you could do better the next time. When you ask for candid feedback, you'll get candid responses. Summarizing what everyone took away from the meeting ensures that you're all on the same page and helps speed follow-up. Ask someone to take notes. Send a quick e-mail to everyone to reinforce what you agreed upon.

When you're embarking on a big project, schedule a meeting to talk things over at the end of each project phase. Doing so will help keep the project on track and allow you to incorporate what you've learned along the way in future phases.

After a while, these debriefing sessions will become second nature. They'll ensure that you are all in sync, provide a template for the next time you roll out a similar project, and keep your team from making the same mistakes twice.

56. Stay in touch.

Whether you're a CEO or a midlevel manager, if you don't regularly talk to customers and clients, you're out of touch. No spreadsheet of suggestions and complaints can sharpen your focus the way a one-on-one conversation can.

One former CEO of a Fortune 500 firm regularly went into the trenches to meet clients at all of the firm's sixty locations. He asked his employees to introduce him to two types of clients: those who needed his help and those who could teach him a thing or two. Whenever clients raised concerns, he addressed them immediately. He called the clients personally when the problem was solved. In doing so, he nipped potentially bigger problems in the bud. His clients loved the personal attention. And thanks to all he'd learned from them, he became a much more effective leader.

No matter how high up in your organization you are, look for ways to get in touch with your company's clients and customers:

- Regularly visit the stores that carry your product or use your services. How did your customers hear about your product? Have they ever been tempted to pick up a rival product instead of yours?
- Attend a local trade show that targets your customers and potential customers. Listen and learn.
- If you're not in sales, ask a sales rep you trust about the customer. What are they hearing on sales calls?
- Set aside one "touch" day each month or quarter to talk with a few key customers or clients. Go straight to the trenches—man the customer service hotline or schedule a lunch with the clients who keep you in business.

When you talk with customers or brokers, don't just focus on your product or service; try to learn a little about their world. Finding out about their goals and fears will build trust and help you serve them better.

When you're working hard—whether you're running the company or managing a busy department or are part of a team developing new projects—it's easy to feel disconnected from the final product and the customer. But you can't focus on the needs of your clients and customers if you don't know what they are. Whether it's on the phone or at a trade show, find some way to "meet" with your customers and ask them about their needs.

57. Master the graceful exit.

Refrain from falling into the trap of running on mindlessly when finishing up a meeting with a client or customer. A colleague recently told me that this was exactly what happened to him during an important sales call. "The meeting had gone well, but for some reason I just kept talking. I could see that I was turning off my prospect. I tried to reengage him, but ended up rambling even more. I was just digging myself deeper into an abyss. All he really wanted me to do was leave his office so he could go to his next meeting."

You're more likely to fall into this trap when you're feeling insecure and the client is an important one. When you've concluded the meeting and discussed all the points you wished to cover, ask the other people you're meeting with if they need anything else from you. If not, recap any next steps you've agreed upon and let them know when they'll be hearing from you again. Then thank them for their time. Close the conversation cleanly with something like "I look forward to working with you," or "Talk to you in a couple of days." Then end the meeting. It's better to end on a high note that you choose, than risk having it end on an awkward or downbeat note.

58. Recognize when it's all been said.

59. Look at the big picture.

Before setting any important goal, it helps to look at the big picture. Many businesses have adopted a technique called a "SWOT analysis" to help them make decisions based on their Strengths and Weaknesses, as well as external Opportunities and Threats. You can do the same in your career. Conducting a "personal SWOT analysis" once a quarter is an easy way to make sure your career is on track.

The first step in conducting a SWOT analysis is to set a clear goal. Perhaps it's the job you want in one year—or in ten. Can you best land that job by staying with your current company or by moving elsewhere? Next, create a list like the one on the next page. Take note of how personal and external factors might affect your goal.

Short-Term Goal: To become the head of a department in the next two years.

Strengths (personal)	Opportunities (external)
I have years of experience and great passion for the work.	Our company is expanding after acquiring another related company.
My boss routinely praises my ability to work effectively with others.	Our industry is becoming more productive as a result of new technology.
I've mastered the skills needed for the job.	
Weaknesses (personal)	Threats (external)
The job I want is currently filled by someone who's been with the company for years and shows no signs of moving on.	Our company is acquiring another related company. (Note that this could be viewed as an opportunity or a threat.)
I haven't headed up a department previously.	The job market is tight.

After looking at the big picture, you might decide to stay with your company. Ask your boss if the acquisition will present any new opportunities. You could also ask your boss to enroll you in a training course on an emerging technology, both to seize new opportunities and to manage any risks the merger might create.

Your goals will likely change over time. That's expected. Just don't lose sight of them. Looking at the big picture will help you understand where you are today—and how to get to where you want to be tomorrow.

60. Know your weaknesses,
but play to your strengths.

Most people focus on their weaknesses and try to improve them. But the most successful executives realize that this is a waste of time. Everyone has strengths and weaknesses, whether they are a CEO or a management trainee. While it's important to be aware of your weaknesses, devoting time and energy to strengthening them will give you only limited gains. You'll become much more effective by building on the things you already do well.

If numbers make sense to you, concentrate on becoming a great numbers person. Yes, you should be able to write a passable business letter. But if that's not your strength, don't invest a great deal of time improving your writing skills or pursuing positions that require a lot of writing. If spreadsheets intimidate you but you have a terrific visual sense, get enough financial literacy training so you can read a balance sheet and understand financial discussions, but invest the majority of your time in developing your design and visual skills. By investing in your natural abilities, you will achieve far more, faster and easier.

A young woman I know shifted careers from acting to management. After initial progress, her career hit a wall. She spent months improving her computer skills and trying to master financial management, with little improvement. One day, while managing a major project, she was asked to make a presentation to an audience of businesspeople. Up to that point, it had been a torturous meeting. But when she took the podium, the room lit up. She entertained and energized the audience, easily gaining their commitment to the project. One of the leaders came up to her afterward and said, "You're great on your feet. You should do more of this." Until then, it had never occurred to her that something that came so naturally to her could be valuable. With her company's help, she began to present more and worked at getting better at it. She was so successful that within a year she was made executive director of a key industry-wide initiative.

One added advantage of playing to your strengths is that they are often where your passions lie. Focusing on your passions will help you push through potential barriers and stay energized when things are difficult. And it makes work a lot more fun.

61. Think three moves ahead.

Effective corporate boards have succession plans that define who will step into key leadership roles when they open up. One reason boards do this is so they can aggressively develop their key talent to ensure they are ready when the time comes—a contingency plan of sorts. They don't have time for up-and-comers to grow organically into more sophisticated executives. So they push the process along. They deliberately put rising stars through various challenges. They place them in varied positions in an organization to help them establish the right relationships, increase their visibility with people, and gain necessary experience in a variety of areas. You can do this for your own career.

Set aside two hours to create a succession plan that identifies the job title or position you want to achieve in five years. On a piece of paper, in separate columns, write down:

1) The positions you need to hold in advance of the position you aspire to
2) The skills and knowledge you need to acquire
3) The experiences you'll need to have under your belt
4) The relationships you'll need to foster to be effective in each position along the way

Review the finished document. Ask yourself if you can really commit to this. Is it achievable? If the answer is yes, then take the first step toward executing your plan. Work with the person you report to in order to master the skills needed to move ahead. Request permission to take on a "stretch assignment," one that requires you to assume new responsibilities and increases your visibility in the organization. Build relationships with the people who can help you move forward. Ask one of them to mentor you, if possible.

If the opportunities you ask for are unavailable at this time, revise your five-year goal and create a realistic plan to help you achieve it. Then make it happen.

Knowing where you want to be and what it will take to get there will greatly increase your chances of success. It will also drastically cut down the time it will take.

62. Know when your career is stuck.

Just as you'll encounter distractions in the course of your day or week, beware of assignments or roles that can burn up years of your career without helping you to grow and advance.

I know one promising young executive who grew so committed to the success of a specific initiative that many years went by before she realized that she was in a dead-end job. Her work was successful, but because there were no positions for her to grow into in her company, she was forced to make a lateral move in order to have a chance to move up.

Your career is stuck when:

- You've become committed to a department's success without knowing how it will benefit your own career.

- You've grown extremely comfortable in your current role, succeeding easily without exerting yourself.
- Everyone comes to you for answers, and you stop learning new things yourself.
- You're happy in your current job but still waiting for an opportunity to present itself that will truly test your resolve. (They rarely present themselves. You need to go out and find them.)
- Your success is overly dependent on one relationship. If that person were to move on, you'd be in trouble.

If one of these applies to you, snap out of it. While it's important to be concerned about the success of your team, your boss, and your company, you can do so while still making sure you're moving ahead in your own career. There is nothing wrong with wanting the best for yourself *and* your company.

63. Make opportunity happen.

A well-seized opportunity can take you farther in a few minutes than months of planning and execution. Throw yourself in its path. Get close to people who've had good things happen to them. Learn from them. If you see a problem, be a part of the solution.

One young professional saw some very troubling things in his organization. Rather than sit back, he analyzed the situation and went straight to his boss. He presented his analysis and said, "Someone needs to recognize we have a problem and lead our team through it." He was given the assignment, excelled at it, and saw his career take off as a result.

Here's how to make opportunities happen:

- Identify the high performers in your company. Work as closely with them as possible. Get on their teams if you can. Follow the careers of the leaders in your industry. Reach out to them when appropriate.

* When new strategies or initiatives are launched in your organization, study them. Watch how they evolve. Look for a way to contribute. Strategic projects are closely watched and can give you a chance to shine.

* Most businesses have an action committee or forum responsible for most of the decision making in the company. Take the ideas you have researched and developed to that committee for consideration. Better yet, become a member.

* When you see a problem, figure out how to fix it. Talk to the people who can do something about it.

* Use business trips wisely. Meet as many people in your industry as you can. You never know when those relationships will become important to your company.

* Be supportive of colleagues. Maintain good relationships with them.

Opportunities don't just materialize out of thin air. You have to reach out and grab them.

64. Delegate.

Effective managers delegate. Your ability to delegate will create ever-increasing amounts of time. It clears the way for you to focus on the important things.

I was once coaching a young financial executive named Joe. Joe had a good-sized staff but didn't effectively use the people he had under him. Worse, although Joe had approval to hire another person for his team, he claimed he was too busy to conduct the interviews. Instead, he worked very long hours, even bringing his kids into the office on the weekends to keep up with the work flow. When I asked him, "Do the people on your team work as many hours as you do?" he answered no. "They need training," he claimed, "and I don't have time to give it to them." And so the cycle continued.

If you find yourself in such a cycle, break it. First, identify a project you can hand off.

1) Look for repetitive projects, like monthly reports, that will give you a long-term return on the time you invest in training someone else to do them. Choose tasks that take you the most time and which others could do.

2) Determine what skills and knowledge are needed to complete the project. Find the person who is the best match.

3) Walk the person through the project the first time. If you think additional training is necessary, arrange to get it for him or her.

4) Make yourself accessible for advice and support, but don't do the work yourself. It's normal for those on your team to be nervous about a new task, but they will feel a sense of accomplishment all the more when they succeed. Praise them when they do.

5) Repeat with other projects and tasks.

With completed projects, it may seem at times as if you could do it faster if you just did it yourself. In fact, that's probably true the first time. The real payoff comes later, when those under you are performing a number of tasks you previously did yourself. And you have more time to do the important work that only you can do.

65. Life is a negotiation.

If you're breathing, you're negotiating. Every day you're trading "this for that"—whether requesting a better compensation package from your employer, negotiating a deal with a client or vendor, or deciding where to dine that evening with your spouse. Make every negotiation a little easier by limiting your wish list to the two or three things that matter most.

Unless you're negotiating a multiyear contract or a peace treaty, don't bring a long laundry list to the table. You're bound to lose something important if you do. I'm not suggesting that you rush negotiations—quite the contrary. Negotiation takes time. Invest it wisely in the important work—knowing exactly what you want, listening to what the other party needs, and envisioning a way to compromise. Don't get caught up in a swap meet of insignificant issues. At best, it's a waste of time; at worst, you risk sacrificing the big issues for the small ones.

Living and working with other people requires a constant give-and-take. Don't damage relationships by haggling over insignificant details. Define the two or three points that matter most. Be willing to lose the rest.

66. Know when to wait.

If the timing isn't right, it doesn't matter how terrific your ideas are or how well you present a case.

I know of a small company that recently experienced a frenzied period of incredible growth. Everyone was working overtime to capitalize on that success and make sure it would continue. One executive, Larry, was working ninety hours a week. About three months into this crunch period, one of Larry's employees asked for a bigger compensation package. Larry was putting in extra hours just to keep the business running. The employee's request fell on deaf ears. The employee didn't get what he wanted. And because he presented himself as someone who missed the big picture, he damaged his relationship with Larry. A year later, when the company was operating at an even keel again, someone else approached Larry with a request for a raise. This time, the timing was right. Because the company had more money, Larry was able to grant her request, offering her a profit-sharing opportunity. Waiting for the right moment paid off.

When people are busy or under pressure, it is not the time to march into their office and ask for a raise. Don't ask your boss to talk about your career goals when he or she is just about to leave for vacation or working on a critical project. When the company has just made a major real estate acquisition, don't try to make a case for a new network. It may seem as if you're wasting time by waiting for the right moment, but you'll get what you want with a lot less effort. And that's cutting to the chase.

67. Know when *not* to wait.

Waiting for approval when it isn't needed wastes your time and everyone else's. It can also slow down your career, making you appear to be unable to make decisions on your own.

Recently, our consulting company received a call from a newspaper editor looking for clarification on some information I'd given him. He was on deadline and needed an answer immediately. Knowing that I was in the middle of a speaking engagement, one of my associates gave him the needed clarification based on her own experience. She later e-mailed me what she'd told him and explained her choice. In point of fact, she had not responded exactly as I would have, but I appreciated that she had the wherewithal to make the call. This kind of confidence excites me. It's a sign of health for both her career and our company.

Strong leaders want people around them with the confidence and courage to take risks. The CEO of a major unit within a global entertainment company recently complained to me that he felt everyone around him was waiting for step-by-step instructions because they were afraid to take risks for themselves. Obviously, there are times when you don't have the authority to make a decision. It's your job to know the difference.

Make a decision when:

* It is clearly within your department or division's responsibility and scope.
* The financial implications are clear and limited.
* You can link your decision to a strategy, goal, or value within your department.

Don't make a decision when:

* It has financial implications beyond your authority.
* It includes a legal issue or compliance dimension.
* It involves your boss's peers or superiors.

A willingness to make decisions is a sign of professional maturity. Don't wait for permission. Analyze the risk and take action.

68. If you need a drummer, hire a drummer.

When he was in college, a colleague of mine put together a band that never quite "made it." When I asked why, he said, "Our drummer was a *great* musician, but his real instrument was piano. He was never good at the drums. But I didn't have the heart to make a change," he said. "Now I know. If you need a drummer, hire a drummer."

The same applies in business. When a small event-production start-up needed a sales VP, they brought in someone who was aggressive, competitive, and charismatic—but who had never worked in sales. His résumé was packed with interesting experiences. He'd even performed on Broadway. The company's executives reasoned that his passion would offset his lack of skill. They were wrong. The company floundered for two years before the CEO made a change. After they hired an *experienced* professional, they were blown away by the difference. Not only did sales increase by 100 percent for the next two years, the new sales VP improved their marketing ROI and sales forecasting.

When you have a job to fill, hire someone with the right skills and experience. Don't fall in love with the name of an impressive company on a candidate's résumé (unless he or she was performing in the right role or position). Don't get so attracted to "extra" skills that you compromise on the required ones. And never hire family or friends unless they are *perfect* for the job. Remember, if you need a drummer—hire a drummer.

69. Don't be afraid to hire people you're going to lose.

One executive had been through so many assistants that she decided to hire someone who would stay in the role long term. As a result, she ended up with a mediocre performer who couldn't keep up. Finally, she tried something different. She hired someone that she was *sure* she would lose eventually—a recent college grad with the right skills, tons of energy, and a great attitude. The executive was honest with the new hire about the nature of the role, but she promised to make the job as valuable as possible for him.

The value this new assistant brought to the table far outweighed the time spent mentoring him. The executive's productivity soared. Of course, it's only a matter of time before the executive will "lose" him as an assistant. But she might gain an associate. And she realized there will always be an eager young grad to take his place.

Employers are often reluctant to hire candidates who want to move up too quickly, for fear of repeating the rehiring and retraining process. Don't be. Hire the person with aspirations and the right skills. They'll be easy to train, will stay motivated, and will help you get a lot more done.

Cut Back

70. Decide what not to do.

When you prioritize, you do what's most important first and put everything else farther down on the list. Sometimes, however, it pays to drop things from your list altogether.

In many Foreign Service schools, students have to pass something called an "inbox exam" before graduating. Students are presented with an inbox of various situations—some crisis level and some less so. They are expected to sort through the inbox and prioritize the work. As they respond to each situation, a group of professors judge their choices. The trick is, there is not enough time to do everything. Beyond deciding what comes first, second, or third, students must decide what to drop completely. A significant part of their grade rests on what they choose to drop.

This is true in any workplace. There is never enough time to do everything. And often, your "grade," whether you work in the executive suite or in a daily support position, depends as much on what you decide *not* to do as what you do.

In determining what to do and what to drop, ask yourself:

* Does it add value to your organization?
* Is it directly linked to a strategic goal?
* Is it critical to ensure that you or your team can do your job effectively?
* Does it directly affect clients or customers?
* Is it teaching you something new and important?

If you answered "no" to the above questions, drop it or delegate it. You'll be more effective at everything else that you do.

71. Addition by subtraction.

We all have them—people who take far more from our lives than they contribute. Whether the person is a friend, a colleague, or someone on your team, find a way to get them out of your life or minimize their impact on it.

One man on a team I was managing was an incredible distraction. He didn't show up to meetings on time. He didn't hit his sales targets. He didn't respond to requests for information. I tried everything I knew to motivate him. Finally, I realized that he didn't want to be motivated. So I let him go. After he left, the entire team changed for the better. You could sense people start to breathe and feel energized again. I realized that I'd waited too long. It had cost me and my team far too much time. It's never easy to fire someone. But experience has taught me that delaying a course of action out of compassion for one man was penalizing the entire team. Nobody was helped by my extended efforts to fix the situation. Moreover, the employee in question went on to find a position with another company. It was a better fit, and he flourished. I learned never to wait again.

I would argue that friends should also enrich your life by challenging you to be your best, giving you honest feedback, supporting your efforts to grow, and standing by you when you're in trouble. If you're not getting this kind of input from the people in your life, do something to change that.

72. Rip it in half.

There's a misconception among businesspeople that the more important your message is, the more time you need to deliver it. I once witnessed someone undermine his career by making a long-winded presentation. Michael had been asked by the new executive vice president in his division to give a fifteen-minute presentation on his strategic thinking about the company's brand position. When Michael handed out his thirty-page PowerPoint deck, I knew we were in for a forty-five-minute presentation. Michael was clearly insecure about how he stood with his new boss. He wanted to show how smart he was. Instead, he exposed himself as an insecure thinker who was unable to express himself in clear terms. Two months later, Michael was gone.

Truman Capote once said, "I believe more in the scissors than I do in the pencil." In any presentation or paper, knowing what to cut is as important as knowing what to include. Whether you are writing reports, speeches, presentations, or even a letter or e-mail, outline everything you think your audience might need to know. Then rip it in half.

How can you tell what to cut? Every report tells a story. Start with an outline of your main arguments. Eliminate everything that doesn't support them. Don't fall in love with extraneous data or detail. If it doesn't add to the "plot," dump it. If you believe readers will need more background information, add an appendix or tell them where they can find it. As you cut, check to make sure your story holds up. When you cannot cut another word without weakening your argument, you're done.

73. The highlighter is mightier than the sword.

My colleagues frequently highlight articles for me. I appreciate the fact that they respect my time and understand my business. But you don't always need a yellow marker to highlight information. Whether you're writing an e-mail to a colleague or making a speech for an audience of 100, you can make your points more pungent by applying the principle of highlighting.

Martin Luther King's "I have a dream" speech is a brilliant example of highlighting in a speech without a marker in sight. His moving repetition of the phrase "I have a dream" is one of the most frequently quoted in literature. But King actually used repetition a number of times—as well as modulating the volume of his voice and underscoring his points through his gestures—to frame the key points of his message.

- He repeated the phrase "*100 years later*" to emphasize the advancements that had yet to occur since Lincoln's Emancipation Proclamation.

- He called out for change by declaring "*Now is the time,*" increasing the volume of his voice with each repetition.

- He admonished his audience, "*We can never be satisfied*" throughout his speech.

- He chanted, "*I have a dream*" again and again as he described his vision of a new America, his voice growing higher and louder, stretching out the word "dream" to emphasize his point.

- And finally, he sang out "*Let freedom ring*" nine times near the conclusion of his speech, underscoring his message.

By using structure, pitch, volume, and gestures as highlighters, King left the hundreds of thousands who listened to his seventeen-minute speech with five key ideas.

There are countless ways to "highlight" key messages in your conversations, memos, presentations, and e-mails. You can use bullets, boldfaced key words, or charts, graphs, or photographs in a PowerPoint presentation. Even the words "And, most important" can indicate to your audience to pay attention. Whatever the medium, define the points that you want your audience or reader to remember. Make them stand out.

74. A picture is worth a thousand words.

Sometimes the right image can instantaneously convey an idea better than any words or phrases. If you want your audience to understand the difference between a small start-up and the fully mature corporate giant, this single picture (on the following page) would outshine a forty-page PowerPoint presentation. If you find yourself wrestling for words that work, consider a picture instead.

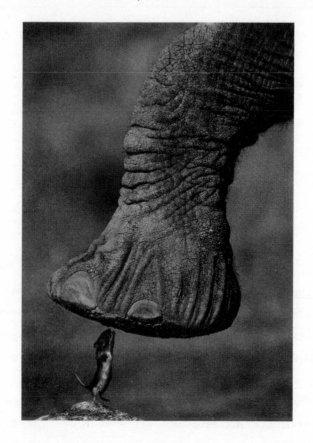

75. Tell a story.

A major client recently said to me, "We have to change to survive. How can we learn to respond as a team when the market throws us a curveball?" Rather than responding with facts and figures, I told her a story of personal survival.

When I was in the U.S. Army, I served as a tank gunner. On one training mission, my commander warned our crew that *any* misfire could be potentially explosive. When, after firing, I heard a "click" instead of feeling the recoil, I called "Misfire!" My commander quickly assessed the situation and saw that the loader had left the safety on. We released it, chose a safe direction to unload the payload, and let it go. The entire transaction took about fifteen seconds. I explained to my client that her company's survival, too, depended on her team members' understanding of their roles, the importance of communication, and the consequences of even the smallest mistake. She got my point immediately.

We often think of storytelling in business as the sole property of "creatives," the marketing and ad whizzes who have proven that there's no faster way to engage people than by spinning a good yarn about a product or service. But it doesn't have to be. Too often the rest of us unflinchingly turn to facts and figures when we want to engage investors, colleagues, and employees when a story would do the trick.

Numbers can help you build a case, but stories drive your message home. The next time you need to make a point or win support for an idea, try presenting it by using a story. If, for example, you want to stress the importance of keeping good people, don't dwell on dry statistics about retention and employee satisfaction. Instead, tell them about Tom, the leader of a successful, but small, company concerned about losing key staff members to a competitor. In response, Tom decided to set up one-on-one breakfasts with each of his fifty-five employees every quarter—he gives them feedback, talks about their goals, and listens to their concerns. In the two years since he started the breakfasts, he's kept every single staff member and grown his business 15 percent.

The next time you're about to whip out the spreadsheets, consider telling a story instead. Give people the chance to identify with another person's struggle and you'll win them over a lot faster.

76. On it. Pending. Done.

Develop a shorthand with your close colleagues. You're all busy, so give each other permission to dispense with the niceties.

One executive uses the words "On it. Pending. Done." with his team. As soon as he sends a request, he receives a response, "On it." If a team member hits a wall, he or she sends a second e-mail with the update: "Pending." If the executive's help is needed, the team members specifically ask for help in a sentence or two. Otherwise, the executive knows it's being handled. When the task is complete, he receives the message "Done."

Another CEO, when he wants someone to move on, e-mails or says "PAC." It stands for "Point accepted. Continue." His team knows it's nothing personal. After all, they're as interested as he is in keeping things moving.

When you're building relationships, you need to clearly communicate your intent and views to ensure they're fully understood. But when you're working with close colleagues, a few words will usually do.

77. . . . To get to the other side.

In meetings, presentations, and reports, it pays to start with the punch line. Give your conclusions before you launch into a detailed explanation. It tells your audience why they should be paying attention and what to look for in the rest of your presentation. Don't make them guess.

Take a look at the last report or review you prepared. Circle the first time you made your point directly. If that circle isn't somewhere in the first two sentences, you waited too long. The only information that should precede your punch line is a short background statement. For example: "During last week's team meeting, you asked me to research new phone-service options." The very next sentence should be "After analyzing the top three options, I recommend that we consider a contract with XYZ vendor for their Premium Plus package." Then lay out your case.

Offering a conclusion after making your case is a bad habit we all picked up in school. In the real world, people want the bottom line up top.

78. Weed out your reading pile.

You can't do your job well if you don't know what's happening in your company, in your industry, in the world. But no one can read a stack of magazines and periodicals the size of Mount Everest. You can't read everything. But you can read *everything you need* by developing a technique for getting the news you need—and nothing else.

Your core reading list should cover these areas:

The broader economic view: Pick one national or global publication—a magazine, a newspaper, or a Web site. Skim the headlines for articles of interest. Read the entire business section.

Your industry: Choose one trade publication. You'll likely find them at work. If not, ask a trusted colleague what to read. When copies arrive, skim them immediately, tearing or printing out any articles that interest you. Most of these publications have a "What's News," "Recent

Deals," or "Intelligence Bytes" section. Pull this out and add it to your reading pile.

Your profession or discipline: Pick a periodical that focuses on advances in your specialty. If you work in information technology for a hotel chain, then, in addition to a hospitality magazine, you should also subscribe to a publication that keeps you up to date with advances in IT. Focus on articles that will help you keep up to date in your job, as well as the next job you hope to get down the line.

Your organization: Every organization has a few reports— from quarterly profits to weekly sales numbers—that provide a wealth of information in a brief snapshot. Though frequently prepared for senior executives, they can almost always be obtained by asking for them. Ask the person who generates the report to add you to the distribution list, as well as to the list for documents detailing the plans or strategies of other departments. When you receive them, print only the executive summaries. Put them in your reading pile.

By now, you've distilled your weekly reading to a manageable size. One day a week, come in an hour early to review the information. Or read them over the weekend for an hour—no more, no less. This kind of reading is not a leisurely activity. Spend no more than five minutes on each piece. Concentrate on what you are reading. Highlight anything you want to remember or share. Finally, never read anything at work outside your core reading list unless it was highlighted for you by a colleague or came from your boss.

79. TMI (too much information).

In many companies, the thirst for data is insatiable. Solid data helps reduce uncertainty and risk, and it promotes quality decisions. But taken to the extreme, information gathering can lead to "analysis paralysis."

One executive with a Fortune 100 company told me: "My direct reports were sending me twenty-five to thirty-page updates each week. And then I'd have a twenty-minute phone call with each of them. When you do the math—I have a dozen direct reports—you see that we spent at least half the week 'feeding the beast.' And my direct reports also report to *another* boss in *another* division whose data requirements are sometimes different from mine. They can conceivably spend 70 to 80 percent of their week doing work that adds no value at all for our customers. I rarely have time to read everything I'm sent.

As a result, the data they assemble isn't even getting applied to our business challenges."

By reducing those weekly reports to two or three pages of information that matter most, the executive is now working to flip this paradigm. His goal is to have his team spend less time writing reports and more time with their *customers*.

Conduct an audit of the different reports that you regularly receive and read. Answer the following questions about each one:

* What is its purpose? Does it achieve its purpose?
* How much time does this take to create?
* Could you achieve your goal with less data? What kind of information is vital?

If people are spending time generating information that doesn't add value to your business, they are wasting your time and theirs. Eliminate unnecessary reports. Streamline those you do need to focus only on useful facts.

80. Good enough is good enough.

There's nothing wrong with wanting to do your best. But striving for perfection when "good enough is good enough" is a waste of time. Don't let unhealthy perfectionism keep you from cutting to the chase. Know when to let things go.

Consider the way new technologies come to market. The major software and electronics companies cut down on time and costs by putting products on the market before they've been completely debugged. Not only does this save the consumer money in the long run; consumer feedback teaches these companies more in a month than they'd discover through years of in-house testing. Sure, some users might grumble at flaws in the early models or releases. But by now, most consumers are aware of the practice and know to wait for the updated version.

You should know when your work is "good enough." Before sitting on or delaying a project or document, ask yourself:

* Will anyone but me appreciate my efforts?
* Can I significantly improve this if I keep working?
* Does the possible gain in quality outweigh the lost time?

If you've answered "no" to the above, wrap it up and move on. If you've answered "yes," map out what still needs to be done and do it—but nothing more.

As Alexander Hamilton said, "I never expect to see a perfect work from an imperfect man." Accept your own imperfection. Do great work in spite of it.

Watch Out

81. Your time is your life.

Don't let other people draw you into taking on their responsibilities. If someone at work asks you to review a document that's only 40 percent complete, tell him or her that your review will be more useful when the document is complete. When you take on someone else's job, you both lose. You lose time. The other person loses the chance to develop his or her abilities and grow in the position.

Value your time. While you should never refuse to help a colleague when the request is warranted, set standards about whom you will go out of your way to invest time in. Invest your time and energy in:

- People who are eager to learn
- People who clearly want to move ahead

- People with passion
- People who respect how busy you are

Your time is your life. When you spend time on things that don't benefit or enrich yourself, you are quite literally wasting your life. Don't allow this to happen. At work and at home, ensure that each moment of your life brings some kind of gain or satisfaction.

Weed out activities that are wasting your time. Every Monday, review your calendar and your "To Do" list. Make a list of activities—including long-standing commitments—you might be able to remove from your schedule. Think about new ways to invest your time. Sign up for a class. Take on a "stretch" project. Spend more time with your family. When you encounter people who tend to eat up your time with little payoff, look for ways to minimize your involvement with them. Respond by e-mail rather than phone to keep interactions short. Have an assistant or team member handle some of the load. Look to add activities into your schedule that are more valuable or offer a better payoff to you and your organization.

None of us can be all things to all people. Figure out what's important in your life. Don't be afraid to pull back from the things that aren't.

82. Don't let your BlackBerry become a CrackBerry.

It's easy to stay connected these days—thanks to cell phones and pagers, Palm Pilots and BlackBerrys that allow us to communicate and access unprecedented amounts of information, wherever and whenever we want. Unfortunately, the frustration of feeling out of touch has been replaced by the burden of a twenty-four-hour day. We've become obsessed with staying connected at all times. If not used wisely, these tools, instead of helping us cut to the chase, can usher in a relentless stream of interruptions in our professional and personal lives. Do you ever find yourself irritated at a fellow commuter who talks nonstop on his cell phone, sharing private and privileged information, while you are attempting to catch up on industry reading? Have you ever been tempted to strangle someone at a meeting who checks his e-mail while others are speaking or presenting?

These productivity tools should serve us, not the other way around. Turn them off when you're in meetings or working on something that involves others or requires concentration. You can check in and respond to e-mails when the meeting or work session is over.

Set an after-hours limit as well—one that works for you, your family, and friends. Make it known that you won't be checking e-mail or voice mail after a certain hour in the evening or on the weekends. Just because technology allows you to receive e-mails twenty-four hours a day doesn't mean you have to accept them. Remember to respect other people's preferences for after-hours communication.

You wouldn't give a hammer or a wrench the power to decide when it will be used. Don't give that power to your phone or PDA, either.

83. Avoid toxic people.

In any organization you'll find what I call toxic people—those whose need for attention distracts everyone else around them. Steer clear of them. They can suck the life out of your day.

One midlevel manager I knew fit this description to a tee. He'd become disgruntled and should have quit, but was high enough up in the organization that he couldn't be easily fired or avoided. He corrupted those around him for months, complaining about unmet expectations, questioning strategy, and making jokes at meetings about the company's practices and those around him. Because he wasn't dangerous enough to be viewed as a threat, he lingered on. He destroyed the morale of half a dozen colleagues before finally leaving to take a new job elsewhere.

Those who were left behind weren't so lucky. It took them over a year to pick up their flagging careers.

You can recognize toxic people by their incessant whining, constant complaints, and need for validation. Don't let yourself get sucked in. If your job puts you in contact with such a person, keep your relationship with them on a strictly professional level. Have as little contact with them as possible. Don't let them taint your reputation by too close an association. Transfer to another department or group, if necessary.

Toxic people are often looking for the courage to quit. Don't let their problem become yours. Keep them at bay and stay on course.

84. Don't let distractions derail you.

In a late-season game, the Dallas Cowboys and the New York Giants were battling for a playoff berth. The Giants took an early lead and were on their way to a second touchdown when they were stopped cold at the thirty-yard line. A field goal would extend their lead and give them some much-needed momentum. But their field goal kicker, Jay Feely, had choked three times in the previous week's defeat. Knowing that Feely would be on edge, Dallas coach Bill Parcells called a time-out to let him feel the pressure and psych him out, a common practice in a high-stakes situation. During the break, the replay screen behind the goalposts showed images of Feely choking in the previous week's game. When the clock started again, Feely lined up, made the kick, and gave the Giants a halftime advantage of 10–0 (they went on to win the game 17–10).

After the game, a television reporter asked Feely about the distraction of seeing last week's botched kicks on the big screen. He replied, "Honestly, I really didn't notice it. I was just focused on making that kick."

That's the kind of focus you need at work to perform consistently at a high level and still have energy left for your personal life. Work environments are filled with distractions. Train yourself to shut them out by conducting what I refer to as a distractions audit. As you review your schedule and "To Do" list before heading home, ask yourself what drew you off course during the day. Are they distractions you can manage—an e-mail solicitation, watercooler talk, a person lingering in your doorway? Write down how you can manage them better next time. Read over this list in the morning to remind yourself that becoming distracted is a choice. Then choose not to let it happen.

85. Don't hang in the door and chat.

You don't appreciate people lingering in your doorway. Others may not want you hanging around theirs. Be respectful of other people's time—and your own. Never stick your head in someone's door and just start to chat. If you do this regularly, others will start to believe you're not working very hard. That can be a tough reputation to overcome.

The next time you drop by a colleague's office with a question or comment, if the other person's hands are on the keyboard, or the phone is in her hand, or she's reviewing a document, you're interrupting. If she doesn't specifically invite you in, move on. E-mail or call her with your question. Or ask the other person to give you a call when she gets a chance. Not everyone will tell you straight out that they're too busy to talk. It's up to you to read the signals and respond accordingly.

If you have some exciting information to share, or need feedback from a colleague, or simply want to bounce a work-related idea off them, do so by e-mail. Or e-mail them a specific request to stop by. If you just need to take a break, take one. Don't inflict your time-out on others around you. Ask a colleague to get some coffee with you. If he can't go, take a short walk yourself. You'll feel more refreshed and work more effectively after a short break than after a longer one spent lingering outside a colleague's office.

86. Cut down on the fire drills.

It's the fifth Friday afternoon in a row that Peter has received an urgent request from Maureen, his team leader. This time, she's frantic about Tuesday's meeting and insists they talk on Sunday to prepare. During the call, she realizes that there's more work to be done and e-mails the entire team with instructions. Everyone's Monday is spent scrambling to get Maureen what she needs. By Tuesday, they're all a day behind in the rest of their work. People were burning out until Peter finally had the courage to ask Maureen to cut down on the fire alarms.

Whether planning for yourself or others, don't wait until the last minute. It throws the situation into crisis mode, killing concentration and productivity. Eventually, it burns people out. Whenever you get an assignment, put aside enough time to get the work done. Establish clear deadlines.

Define the steps you'll need to take to reach your goal. Then stick to them.

Of course, there will always be urgent matters that require you to drop everything else. But if everything's an emergency, nothing is. Respect yourself and the people around you by planning ahead and eliminating unnecessary fire drills.

87. Know when you're stuck.

If you've started to write the same sentence five times, stop. If no one in the meeting is budging on the negotiation point, stop. If you keep putting off an important task and don't know why, stop. When you're stuck, you're stuck. Spinning your wheels won't help. You need to dig your way out of the mud.

Ask yourself:

1) Do I have enough information?
2) Can someone else's input help move this forward quickly?
3) Do I/we have the authority to move forward?
4) Can I come at it from a different perspective?
5) Am I simply afraid to make a decision?

Whether you're working alone or in a group, asking these questions will almost always help you to move forward. If you need more information to make a decision, postpone things until you get it. If the right people aren't involved, seek them out. If you need a new perspective, bring in an outside opinion.

Maria, one of my firm's clients, was leading a successful strategic initiative in a $4 billion company. My colleague Liz, who was supporting her on the project, suggested several times that Maria brief the CEO in order to start building the support she would need for additional resources later in the year. Maria always seemed to have a delaying tactic: "After we have the full plan in place," she would say, or "After we've made more progress." Finally, Liz asked, "Why don't you want to brief the CEO? The project is going beautifully." Maria said candidly, "I guess I'm afraid. I've heard that he can be unpredictable." Liz persuaded her to meet with several people who regularly briefed the CEO to get their advice on the best way to approach such a meeting. She followed their advice. The project's budget was approved later that year.

Recognizing when you're stuck can help you to move forward. Don't let yourself just spin your wheels.

88. When you hear something once, pay attention. When you hear it twice, act.

We waste a lot of time ignoring criticism and warnings because it makes us uncomfortable. We don't want to believe the worst, or else fear confronting it. For example, most heart attack victims ignore initial warning signs, attributing them to heartburn or stress. By not checking with a physician about their symptoms, they put themselves at risk for permanent heart damage, or worse. It's a powerful example about the human desire to ignore warning signs.

If two customers leave a restaurant you own because the food is cold, or you get called out at work for being unprepared for a meeting several times, you're doing something wrong. When you get feedback about yourself more than once, that's a trend. If you hear a similar comment twice within a relatively short period of time, that's an urgent trend. Remember, frequency of repetition is what gives researchers confidence in their results. They realize that the more often you hear something, the more likely it is to be true.

So listen carefully to feedback from others. Thank the people who give it to you. Then fix the problem.

89. If you sense trouble, do something.

Even small misunderstandings can snowball into conflicts. It's up to you not to let these snowballs turn into avalanches.

Recently, an IT executive was asked to build a program to support one of his company's departments. Even after a number of meetings, he'd made no progress with the program. People were getting frustrated. The company's president sensed something was amiss. He assumed someone would bring it to his attention if the issue was important enough. Instead it bubbled beneath the surface, distracting the entire team for months.

In the meantime, the company experienced a leadership transition. When the new president sensed a problem, she brought in the IT exec to get a status report. When the IT exec admitted he had no idea where things stood, the new president talked to a few team members. She discovered that they were furious and resentful about the lack of leadership. She immediately clarified roles and responsibilities without assigning any blame, defined how the project's success would be measured, and established biweekly reporting sessions about the project. She turned things around quickly, but the company had already lost six months of time to rambling meetings and unabated water-cooler rantings. If you were to calculate the lost productivity, it would easily top $100,000, and all because no one stepped up to solve the problem.

The minute you see confusion or conflict about to snowball into something bigger, face it head-on. Avoid blaming and finger-pointing, which only make things worse. Problems rarely resolve themselves. Until someone stops them, they only get bigger.

90. Procrastination takes years off your life.

In an appearance on ABC's *20/20*, anti-aging specialists Dr. Michael Roizen and Dr. Mehmet Oz—coauthors of the best-selling *You: The Owner's Manual*—revealed that not every kind of stress causes premature aging. The stresses that cause health problems are not pressing deadlines, sudden crises, or a demanding boss. The stresses that are most hazardous are those "Nagging Unfinished Tasks" that Roizen and Oz call "NUTs."

"One nagging unfinished task . . . puts approximately eight years on your life. So if you're thirty, it makes you thirty-eight," said Roizen. Talk about an opportunity to gain back the gift of time! Many of the recommendations in this book will help you tackle those unfinished tasks. But we all know there are days when you can't finish everything. Learning how to cope with *not* getting everything done is just as important as getting more done.

When you're feeling swamped, here are some simple ways to decompress:

- Bend and breathe: Whether you attempt sophisticated yoga postures or just do simple stretching and breathing at your desk, the benefits are undeniable.
- Laugh: Nothing releases stress better.
- See friends: Those who see six friends or more a month are happier and healthier over the long term.

Your first line of defense against NUTs is to tackle each task immediately. But when things pile up—as unmercifully they inevitably will—take a deep breath, laugh, and remember all the things outside of work that you're working for.

91. Don't confuse activity with accomplishment.

Don't confuse being busy with being productive. Or as one manager I know puts it, "WORK = FORCE × DISTANCE. Your team can spend the whole day pushing against the Empire State Building, but if they don't *move* it, they didn't do any work." While this theorem originally applied to physical work, it can be applied to any kind of effort. If you didn't get anything measurable done, then you didn't do any work.

Here are a few strategies to turn activity into accomplishment:

- *Learn from the past.* Think about the last time you faced a similar task. What helped you achieve results? Start with that.
- *Ask an expert.* If there's someone in your organiza-

tion or a colleague in your field who has had success on a similar project, get their advice.

- *Track the relationship between your efforts and your results.* Don't just count the number of brochures you sent out or the number of calls you made. Track the number of leads each activity generated. Instead of thinking only about what you are doing to improve customer service, pay close attention to how your work is directly affecting customer satisfaction numbers. Over time you'll start to see which of your activities get the best results.

If you performed tasks all day but accomplished nothing, you did no work. You only wasted time and energy. Keeping track of what's worked in the past is the fastest way to achieve success now.

92. Don't make the same mistake twice.

If you're making a lot of different mistakes, you're learning. If you're making the same mistakes more than once, you're wasting time. Successful people learn from their mistakes right away and don't repeat them.

An entrepreneur I know tried to cut corners by paying a college student, rather than a professional, to clean the office carpets. The student absentmindedly left a faucet running over the weekend. When the entrepreneur came in on Monday, the office had flooded. Later that year, when relocating, he made a similar mistake by hiring some inexpensive laborers instead of reputable movers. When they damaged some expensive computer equipment (of course, they had no insurance to foot the cost), the entrepreneur asked, "Why do these things always happen to me?" They happened to him because he didn't learn from his mistake the first time.

Keeping a "lessons learned" file is one way to avoid making the same mistake twice. Whenever something goes wrong, take a minute to figure out why. Do you see a pattern? If you're not sure what went wrong, you may want to ask someone you trust for advice.

Analyzing your mistakes will take some of the sting out of what's happened, give you a sense of control, and help you avoid similar missteps down the line. Whenever you're preparing for a major meeting, appointment, or presentation, consult your file to remind yourself of lessons you've learned.

If you're making mistakes, you're trying new things and growing. Don't beat yourself up about them. Learn quickly and move on.

93. Sweat the small stuff.

When you cut to the chase, don't forget the little details. When ignored, the "small stuff" has a habit of turning into big problems.

A company I know had invited several prospective clients to a basketball game at Madison Square Garden. Each client received directions to the meeting place and—because Madison Square Garden can be hard to navigate—the marketing manager's cell phone number. Sure enough, a major prospect did get lost. But instead of wandering around feeling frustrated, he called the cell phone number and was promptly escorted to the gathering.

Run through a checklist such as the one below every Monday morning. It will take only a few minutes, but it might save you from losing an important account or client—or even your job.

- What meetings do I have scheduled this week? Have they all been confirmed? Do I have the specific locations and cell phone numbers I need? Do I have time to get from one meeting to the next? If it's my meeting, have I reserved space and sent the agenda?
- Do I have all the materials and tools necessary for the week?
- Have I reminded my team of everything I'll need from them this week—and when I expect it? Is anything major happening this week—such as advertising promotions or a seasonal increase in business—that they should be aware of?
- Are my audiovisual needs arranged for presentations? Do I need to make copies of anything? If so, how many?
- Are all travel arrangements finalized, printed out, and filed with materials for the trip? If I'm going to be out of reach, have I informed everyone?
- Is my PDA in sync with my system?

Fill in these gaps and face the week confident that the small stuff is covered. Then focus on the big stuff.

Find Balance

94. Don't let a difficult coworker dominate your life.

When Jean-Paul Sartre said, "Hell is other people," I think he was specifically referring to difficult coworkers. When you work with someone who is hard to please, easy to anger, or quick to criticize, every request can feel like pulling teeth, every encounter like stepping in a minefield.

Don't throw up your hands in despair. If the difficult person in question is your boss, explain that you're eager to work hard but that yelling, backbiting, or harsh criticism decreases your motivation. If he or she doesn't respond, let it go. Start looking for another job right away.

What if leaving isn't an option? Maybe the job market is tight or the person giving you trouble is just one colleague, client, or customer out of many? If you have difficulty with a coworker but love your job, here are some ways to keep it—and your sanity:

- Accept his or her style. You can't change other people. It wastes your emotional energy to try.
- Don't take it personally.
- Don't waste valuable time complaining about your colleague.
- Minimize the time you spend with the person. Define exactly what you need from him or her. Get it as quickly as possible, preferably by e-mail.
- Learn what you can from them. Difficult people often get away with bad behavior because they excel at something. If he or she is a brilliant salesperson or an exceptional designer, learn as much from the situation as you can.
- If the problem worker is your boss, and he or she isn't helping to increase your visibility in the organization, make your contributions known. Announce key projects, volunteer for cross-departmental teams, participate enthusiastically in meetings, and talk with colleagues about your ideas.

Most important, keep on doing excellent work. It will improve your self-esteem, accelerate your ability to win a promotion, or facilitate your search for another job. Difficult people are a pain in the pants. But if you're good at your job, no amount of petty or incompetent behavior can hold you back.

95. Manage your personal life as well as your professional life.

It's not enough to use this book to improve your professional habits. You also need to change the way you approach your personal life. What's the point of keeping detailed expense reports at the office if you need to tear your house apart just to find a bank statement? Why bother scheduling meetings all week long if you forget to buy your daughter tickets to the sold-out playoff game on Saturday? Why work so hard all week if you ignore everything you're working for?

Here are a few examples of ways to cut to the chase in your personal life.

Bills	If you're not already using electronic bill payment and direct deposit, start now. Remember to review bank and credit statements once a month.

Records management	Establish a filing system to manage financial records. Accounting software like Quickbooks can help. Just make sure to back up files—a few seconds today can save you weeks of work later on.
Errands	Do all your errands—dry cleaning, groceries, etc.—at once. Keep a list of frequently purchased items. Look into grocery-delivery services or dry cleaners who pick up.
Friends, hobbies, exercise	Make weekend plans ahead of time so you don't get locked out. If you choose to play it by ear, be ready to improvise.

You can't be your best at work if your personal life's a mess. Stay on top of things so they don't pile up. Your family and your boss will thank you.

96. Renew yourself every day.

A person should hear a little music, read a little poetry, and see a fine picture every day in order that worldly cares may not obliterate the sense of the beautiful which God has implanted in the human soul.

—Goethe

Goethe wasn't suggesting that you block out half the day to escape to the mountains. He understood that it is possible to invigorate your body, mind, and spirit in just a few minutes each day. It will give you a fresh perspective on your work and life, energize you, and increase your focus.

If you can't see the point of renewing yourself, perhaps you need a reminder of what you're missing. Write down three words—*mind, body,* and *spirit*—on one side of a piece of paper. Across from each, jot down some ways you could revitalize yourself in those areas. (Some may overlap.) Here's an example:

Mind	Read a book, have a good conversation with someone outside my field, visit a museum.
Body	Go to the gym, stretch, walk, do yoga, get a massage, sleep, drink plenty of water.
Spirit	Meditate, study, pray, garden, play the piano, put photos of my family on the desk.

Strive to dedicate a few minutes each day to renewing your mind, body, and spirit, whether you spend twenty minutes reading a book or an hour at the gym.

If you constantly put off renewing yourself for that week away at Canyon Ranch, you'll find yourself disappointed forty-nine weeks out of the year. Don't wait for a vacation. Make self-renewal an essential part of each day.

97. Take back the weekend.

It's 4:30 on Friday afternoon. You're ready to go home. After putting out fires all week, you're the one who's burned out. But you've got a pocketful of business cards, a pile of receipts to sort through, and at least three people waiting to hear back on something. You decide to go home anyway and "catch up" over the weekend.

Stop!

Unlike on weeknights—when your goal is to clean up quickly and respond to anything time-sensitive—Friday afternoons are the time to close *every* open loop and catch up on those easy-to-put-off tasks that clutter your desk and mind.

Before you leave the office, make sure you've delivered on promises, reviewed everything that needs your input, and returned all calls and e-mails. Stay late if you need to.

Better yet, set aside time earlier in the day so you don't have to. Then start climbing the mountain one issue, one response at a time. Start with the simple things to build a little momentum. Work your way to the tougher tasks. Not only will you be better able to enjoy your time off, your colleagues will appreciate that you're eliminating bottlenecks that result from holding on to their proposals or e-mails.

Starting the weekend with a clear conscience will liberate you to enjoy two worry-free days and begin the following week with a clean slate. I know that some of you don't want to give up your 4:00 A.M. Sunday e-mail exchanges. That's your choice. This book is for people trying to make a different choice: to take back their time.

98. Turn the page.

Sometimes it's hard to detach from work when you leave for the day. Some people need an entire evening to unwind, and others never really let go. But to be your most productive during the day, you need time away from work to recharge your physical and emotional batteries. When you leave work, spend the last five to ten minutes organizing your work area or office for the next day. Don't get sucked into working. Just clear your desk and put things where they belong. Make the choice to "turn the page." You can accelerate this process by creating a routine that reinforces the fact that work is over and you're off the clock. Do it every evening before you head home.

Your routine should start at your desk or work area. Fifteen minutes before you go, check your e-mail and voice mail. Respond to any that are time-sensitive and, beyond that, as many as you can fit in comfortably.

As you travel home, make a mental list of things you'd like to do for yourself, with your friends or family that evening. Start planning for the other part of your life.

Before or when you arrive home, take a minute or two to return any last-minute e-mails or phone calls, if necessary. Then turn off your cell phone, your computer, and, if you have one, your PDA. Yes, there may be an occasional evening when you need to be available to colleagues or clients. If you're preparing for a big meeting or have a major project looming, you need to keep your PDA on. But even if you are the CEO, don't make this the norm.

Don't spend time dwelling on work issues. If something is bothering you, write it down so that you don't forget it, or leave yourself a voice mail at work. Then let it go. When you need to blow off a little steam to your spouse or a friend about something from work that's bothering you, put a fifteen-minute time limit on it. Beyond that, you're giving away the time for yourself and your loved ones that you've been working so hard to gain back.

99. Know when to put the book down.

If you've grown irritable or are snapping at people, if you're exhausted or can't focus, if you can't fall asleep or are waking up in the middle of the night, take a step back. It's time to do more than "turn the page" on a workday. You need to put the book down. Whether it's a long weekend or a true vacation, you need a break. Your fatigue is affecting your work and your relationships. Things aren't going to improve until you take some extended time off to reenergize.

As soon as you confirm your time off, start planning. You're not doing yourself or your colleagues any favors by waiting until the day before you leave. No one wants to hear a person on the elevator complaining about how stressful it is to take a vacation. More important, no one wants to pick up the slack for you because you didn't plan ahead.

As soon as you schedule your time off:

- Alert everyone you work with regularly.
- Make a list of the work you need to wrap up before your break. Determine what to postpone.
- Make a list of your projects or tasks due while you're gone. Select people to cover for you. Meet with them to make sure they have everything they need.
- Update your boss on where things stand. Let him or her know who will be covering for you. (If your boss is comfortable when you walk out the door, you will be, too.)

Then take your time off. Depending on your job, you may need to check in occasionally. But have faith in your colleagues. Let them know how to contact you in an absolute emergency. Ask them to handle everything else on their own. Allow your team to grow while you renew.

100. A bottle of wine, a cut flower.

The intense discipline of staying focused on the goals in your life and career will result in more time for yourself, your family, and the things you enjoy. That is the payoff of cutting to the chase.

A friend of mine recently retired from a highly successful career with a Fortune 500 company. Incredibly intense, he never developed outside interests because he was so focused on his business. As he adjusted to retirement, I could tell he needed something new. So I took him to the wine store to introduce him to the joys of fine wine. He loved it. Today he is learning about vintages and wine-growing regions. His wife tells me that it's the best thing I could have done for him. He is like a man reborn. And sharing something I love in life with a friend is the kind of moment I work for when I push hard through the week.

Similarly, I love to garden. Our yard is filled with flowers for three quarters of the year. I love the feeling of being close to nature, the power and beauty of it. I like the fact that the garden changes every day. I try to observe those changes as they occur. I can see when a rose is about to bloom. I try to make time each day to watch it unfold. When the first flowers come out in the spring, I wash out all the vases in the house and cut flowers to put around my house. It's my gift to myself and to my wife, Harriet. We work hard, and these are the moments that we work for. Time at my home with my wife and my kids when they're home from college. Time to care for ourselves.

Be mindful of these moments. Cherish them. They will renew you and help you sustain the intense discipline necessary to thrive in your career—and hopefully other parts of your life.

Move past the page and into action.

While cutting to the chase can give you back hours of time each week, ironically, it does require an up-front investment of time. Start by scheduling time to train yourself to cut to the chase. Eventually, these habits will become second nature in both your professional and personal life.

I suggest tackling one rule per day. Why? Because you want to challenge yourself without burning out. If you were joining a gym, your trainer would not only encourage you to push yourself, but also to listen to your body so you don't overdo it. Similarly, I recommend setting the bar high by focusing on a new rule each day, while paying attention to whether or not you're making *real* change. If you start to feel overwhelmed by your effort to improve, take a step back and spend a few days on the rule that's challenging you. When you've mastered it, move on.

Where to begin? That's your choice. If you're losing two hours a day to people dropping by your office, then "Create a no loitering zone" should be high on your list. If your boss hints that you need to get to the point faster, consider "Rip it in half" or "Think in bullets." Keep in mind that some of these rules are more "action-oriented," while others require clear thought. Some rules should become daily habits. You may need to call upon others only periodically.

On the next page, I've provided a sample monthly calendar as a guide to help you to cut to the chase. Each day includes a rule or a concept from a rule that I have made part of my routine. We recommend that certain rules be done daily, weekly, monthly, or quarterly, and these are placed on the calendar in brackets. Others are left blank intentionally because they are personal. Of course, this is only a guide. Your own Cut to the Chase Calendar should reflect the rules *you* feel will help you the most to gain back the gift of time.

January 2008

MONDAY	TUESDAY	WEDNESDAY	THURSDAY	FRIDAY	SATURDAY	SUNDAY
	1 New Year's Day	2 "Get in early and go home on time."	3 Use "The first 20 minutes" to focus the day. [daily]	4 Ask for everything needed before the weekend. ("Take back the weekend.") [weekly]	5 Find time and place to reflect upon my life's purpose. ("Every second counts.")	6 Spend the afternoon with kids. ("A bottle of wine, a cut flower.")
7 Review week ahead and make sure "small stuff" is covered. [weekly]	8 Make plans for the weekend. ("Manage your personal life as well as your professional life.") [weekly]	9 Take walk at lunch, listen to music on commute home, read novel after dinner. ("Renew yourself every day.") [weekly]	10 End day by scanning calendar to make sure all objectives were met. ("Start with the end in mind.") [daily]	11 Look over "To Do" list for project to "Delegate."	12 Take Harriet to a show. ("A bottle of wine, a cut flower.")	13 Leave pen and paper by bed at night to record nagging issues. ("What's keeping you up night?") [daily]
14 Estimate time projects will take on "To Do" list. ("Predict how long things take.")	15 "Explode out of the blocks" by doing something energizing before work. [daily]	16 Organize workspace. ("Organize yourself first.")	17 "Think in bullets" all day. [daily]	18 Work on reducing size of all documents. ("Rip it in half.")	19 See friends from outside professional life for dinner. ("Manage your personal life as well as your professional life."). [weekly]	20 "Conduct personal SWOT analysis" to ground career direction. ("Look at the big picture.") [quarterly]
21 Think about what to cut from schedule to focus on important things. ("Decide what not to do.")	22 Conduct a distractions audit. ("Don't let distractions derail you.") [weekly]	23 Evaluate "What's been going better lately and why." [quarterly]	24 Tackle at least one Nagging Unfinished Task. ("Procrastination takes years off your life.") [weekly]	25 "Weed out reading pile." [weekly]	26 Get all errands done by 12 P.M. ("Manage your personal life as well as your professional life.") [weekly]	27 Get personal accounting program loaded and download bank statements. ("Manage your personal life as well as your professional life.")
28 Review actual time things took vs. estimated time. ("Predict how long things will take.")	29 Create "lessons learned" file. ("Don't make the same mistake twice.") [weekly]	30 "Stay in touch" by meeting with a key customer. [monthly]	31 Before leaving work, spend the last 5–10 minutes organising your work area for the next day. ("Turn the page.")			